BRITISH COAL

The Rugby League Yearbook

1989–90

D0314536

BRITISH COAL

The Rugby League Yearbook
1989–90

The Kingswood Press

The Kingswood Press
an imprint of Methuen London
Michelin House, 81 Fulham Road, London SW3 6RB

Copyright © The Kingswood Press except for
the 1989–90 fixtures which remain the
copyright © 1989 The Rugby Football League

First published 1989
ISBN 0 413 62470 6

Photoset, printed and bound in Great Britain
by Redwood Burn Limited, Trowbridge, Wiltshire

Contents

Acknowledgements

With eleven exceptions, the photographs in this book have
been reproduced by kind permission of Andrew Varley. The
exceptions are those on pages 78, 81, 90, 112, 114, 115 and
117, which are reproduced by kind permission of *Open
Rugby* magazine, that on page 89 by permission of Peter
Arkell, and those on pages 135, 140 and 141 have been
generously supplied by *The News*, Christchurch, New Zealand.

Not for the first time the publishers are indebted also to Mike
Rylance for his generous help and guidance.

Preface

David Oxley OBE
Chief Executive, the Rugby Football League

Future generations will undoubtedly see the 1988–89 season as one rarely, if ever, equalled and, surely, never bettered in terms of quality of play and the high level of entertainment achieved. It was, then, no coincidence that for the second season in succession attendances rose by a massive 25 per cent. Nowhere was the champagne spirit of the season more in evidence than at Widnes, superlative winners for the second season in succession of both the first division championship and the premiership. Halfway through the season, they added to the dazzling array of talent the brilliant potential of Jonathan Davies whose signing gave rise to unprecedented publicity for the game at national and indeed international level. It is a wonderful prospect for the game, though no doubt daunting for the opposition, that we have yet to see the best from this quite outstanding Naughton Park outfit, though mighty Wigan beat them in the John Player final, won the Lancashire Cup and scored a second successive totally comprehensive victory at Wembley. Elsewhere, the whole game rejoiced in Sheffield's proud performance in winning promotion and taking the second division premiership, the fruition of five years of inspired hard work by all who have served the Eagles so well.

The early part of the season saw the opening of Rugby League's Hall of Fame and a thoroughly entertaining and competitive match between Great Britain and the Rest of the World XIII to celebrate the induction of the first nine immortals, whose illustrious careers exhibited the highest standards of skill and sportmanship, courage and class. Such qualities, of course, must be deeply bedded in strong grassroots and to this end the Rugby League Foundation has guaranteed the amateur game £1 million for development over the next three years. Last season saw the number of full-time regional development officers rise to thirteen, including appointments in London and in the vitally important area of Student Rugby League.

I am delighted that British Coal's sponsorship of international football over the next four years will begin with what is bound to be an epic Test series between Great Britain and New Zealand this autumn. Already generous sponsors both of this *Yearbook* and of youth football, our friends from British Coal have rapidly become numbered amongst the game's staunchest supporters and greatest benefactors. We are proud to be associated with them: they will not be disappointed.

Foreword

Martin Cruttenden
Director of Sales, British Coal Corporation

Coal and Rugby League have always been closely associated and British Coal's involvement with the sport now reaches from the game's grassroots to the highest level of them all – international Rugby League.

Both Rugby League and British Coal used to be unfairly saddled with an inaccurate image of being old-fashioned and rather dirty. Not any more. 'The New Face of British Coal' has created new uses and new markets for one of Britain's prime sources of energy, while Rugby League has become the fastest, most skilful, most spectacular contact sport in the world.

As the sport has reached new peaks of excellence, attendances have boomed and the exciting spectacle of the game on television has brought Rugby League out of the shadows into the national spotlight. Rugby League is played at amateur level throughout the country, while plans for a truly national network of professional clubs are far advanced.

At every level, British Coal is fostering this growth. They contribute to the Rugby League Foundation by channelling money into the development of the game at school, youth and amateur levels, financing centres of excellence, advanced training programmes, travel grants and general development work. The British Coal National Youth League is a logical extension of this policy, an elite Under-19 competition involving the cream of young Rugby League players from all over the country.

This development programme, aided by British Coal, should ensure a steady flow of top-class young players into the professional game in the years to come. Some of them will go on to achieve the ultimate honour – selection for Great Britain – and at international level, too, British Coal is supporting Rugby League. Great Britain face Test series against all four of the leading international countries during 1989 and 1990 and in all of them, and for at least the next four years, British Coal will be sponsoring the Great Britain side.

I

The 1988–89 Season
At Home

ONE

The Stones Bitter Championship and Premiership Trophies

Trevor Watson

THE STONES BITTER CHAMPIONSHIP

The crowd explodes at Martin Offiah's hat-trick, and Widnes are nearly home in the championship decider against Wigan.

It was as if the climax to the Stones Bitter Championship had been stage-managed. Eight months of league rugby were encapsulated into a final, fascinating eighty minutes at Naughton Park, between the top two teams, the champions Widnes and the challengers Wigan, the winners to take the title; little wonder that all 16,000 tickets had been snapped up. It was a true championship final. Widnes were a point ahead in the table and a draw would be enough for them to retain the title. But no one was even thinking about a draw; it would be victory or nothing.

The Chemics, of course, had home advantage, but were playing their tenth game in thirty-two days and for some of the team the strain had begun to tell. Wigan were on a superb run of sixteen successive wins, but were without their half-back linchpins, Andy Gregory and Shaun Edwards. Yet tries by Andy Platt and Andy Goodway and goals by Joe Lydon gave Wigan a 12–4 lead after twenty-six minutes, with Martin Offiah having scored a try for Widnes.

Widnes beat Wigan 26–12 to end a magnificent season. The championship trophy is theirs and Martin Offiah, Kurt Sorensen and Barry Dowd do not intend to let it go.

That try was a sign of things to come. Offiah scored again and, with Jonathan Davies adding a goal, the gap was down to 2 points at the interval, with the game and the title still very much in the balance. Then the Chemics exploded and took command with three tries in nine blistering minutes early in the second half. A sparkling run by Alan Tait enabled Kurt Sorensen to crash over and the home men were ahead. Then came a magnificent try by Offiah, who sliced between Tony Iro and Dean Bell and held off Steve Hampson and Mark Preston to complete his hat-trick and register his fifty-fourth try of the season. When Paul Hulme charged over by the posts, it seemed all over at 26–12 to Widnes, but still the season refused to fade away.

Widnes had Emosi Koloto sent off for a high tackle, Ellery Hanley swept in for a typical try and suddenly Wigan were back in the hunt, though still trailing 18–26. Could the twelve Widnes men hang on to their lead and the title? They not only did, but four minutes from the end Phil McKenzie darted in for the sixth Widnes try and Davies added his fourth goal to keep the title at Naughton Park with a 32–18 triumph after a great finale to an absorbing season.

The general feeling at the outset was that it would be the toughest first division since the two-division system was restored in 1973. There was no obviously weak side among the fourteen clubs and it was clearly going to be just as tight at the bottom as at the top. Widnes lost their opening game at Halifax and soon afterwards were beaten at Salford. In between they hammered Hull, Leeds and Featherstone Rovers and their pace was apparent as Offiah twice collected four tries, Rick Thackray scored a hat-trick at Leeds and Andy Currier scored five against Rovers.

Castleford soon emerged from the pack, putting together a fine run and, with Widnes and Wigan involved in the John Player Trophy, the Yorkshire side stretched their lead, staying unbeaten in the league until 8 January. Then they lost to the bottom club, Halifax, to underline again that there were no easy matches in the first division. Yet the title seemed to be in Castleford's hands for the first time in their sixty-two year history until it all went horribly wrong and they went nine games without a win, to slip out of the top four.

Leeds had a spell at the top, but the chasing teams had games in hand and Widnes became favourites with Wigan hovering at their heels. March was a fascinating month as both Widnes and Wigan continued to make up ground. Then Widnes crashed at home to Bradford Northern, who were in danger of relegation, and lost at Hull, and the race was really on.

The Championship went into its final week with Widnes, Leeds and Wigan still in contention. Widnes won hair-raising games at Hull KR (16–13) and Castleford (24–22) to end Leeds's hopes, and more than 21,000 saw Wigan's incredible run continue with a narrow victory over St Helens to set the scene for that fabulous final day.

Widnes probably deserved the title for the quality of their rugby. They were the only first-division side to top 700 points and had the best defensive record. Offiah continued to thrill the crowds. He still had his critics but if a player tops 100 tries inside two seasons, his defence is incidental. David Hulme returned from the Lions tour a very accomplished player in both half-back positions, Sorensen was still a respected figure, McKenzie looked the best hooker around and Koloto was a sensation in his first season of Rugby League in

Britain. There was the solid professionalism of such as Derek Pyke, Joe Grima, Mike O'Neill, Richard Eyres and the often unsung Paul Hulme, while Tait became the best attacking full-back in the league.

The solid professionalism of Richard Eyres was an important ingredient in the all-round quality of the rugby Widnes played throughout the season.

Widnes also, of course, attracted national attention, when their coach, Doug Laughton, used his powers of persuasion to win the signature of the Wales Rugby Union captain, Jonathan Davies. It irked Rugby League men to see Widnes described in terms of the chemical works as if all Union grounds were nature reserves and there were no chimneys in Wales.

However, Davies withstood the welter of publicity with patient good humour. Inevitably his failings were picked out before he had kicked a ball. He was carefully, perhaps too carefully, nursed along but when the title was won he could look back on 89 points in seven games as his contribution – and his

Widnes's signing of Jonathan Davies,
the Welsh Rugby Union captain,
won the game more national
publicity than practically any other
event during the 1988–89 season.

Adrian Shelford, Wigan's New Zealand prop, enjoyed another excellent season in the championship.

head was still on his shoulders. Just to keep things ticking over, Laughton then returned to Wales and signed the second row, Paul Moriarty, from Swansea RU to revive talk of a Welsh national RL team.

Wigan were left wondering what might have happened had they not elected to play matches when they had men away on World Cup final duty in New Zealand as well as out with injuries, although the decision did prevent a fixture pile-up. Hanley had a great season, looking the complete professional. While Gregory and Edwards had brief fall-outs with their coach, Graham Lowe, his strict code won the argument and both produced some fine performances. Adrian Shelford was another to have an excellent season as did his fellow prop, the up-and-coming Ian Lucas, while Dennis Betts seems certain to be in contention with Lucas for Great Britain honours in the near future. It's worth recalling that Wigan went almost the whole season without Henderson Gill, but still had a quality threequarter line in which Kevin Iro was particularly impressive. Consolation for finishing second was a record average gate of more than 15,000.

Leeds began with high optimism under their new coach, Malcolm Reilly, and followed the previous season's spending spree by signing the Great Britain tourists, Hugh Waddell, Paul Dixon and Phil Ford, in addition to the England Rugby Union threequarter, John Bentley, who settled in smoothly. There were also three Australians in the exciting Andrew Ettingshausen, the stand-off Cliff Lyons, and the heavyweight prop Sam Backo. Ettingshausen again delighted the fans and there was solid effort from Lyons, but Backo never adjusted to the looser style of the British game. Leeds's scoring star, Garry Schofield, missed two important months in mid-season because of a damaged shoulder and took time to settle on his return. The club also produced a promising youngster in scrum-half Paul Delaney. Attendances at Headingley rose to more than 12,000 to indicate their potential should they begin to win major trophies regularly.

For Hull to finish fourth was a tremendous effort. They were expected to struggle, and four opening defeats gave no reason to change that view. But their new Australian coach, Brian Smith, worked wonders with his squad and they became a very sound outfit, superbly led by the Australian scrum-half, Craig Coleman, and the second row, David Boyle. It says much for the organisation and spirit at the Boulevard that the return of Coleman and Boyle to Australia at the beginning of March did not affect the teamwork. Prop Andy Dannatt and hooker Lee Jackson made great progress and Tim Wilby adjusted easily from centre to second row. Their Welsh stand-off, Gary Pearce, was shaken by being left out for some time, but came back well and developed into a key man, his goal and tactical kicking being first-rate.

Phil McKenzie looked the best hooker around through the long championship season and it was fitting that he should be among Widnes's try-scorers in the championship decider against Wigan.

The three outstanding coaches of the 1988–89 season were surely (*left to right*) Graham Lowe, who announced his return to Australia (in fact, to Manly) after three hugely successful years at Wigan; Peter Fox, who took Featherstone Rovers to sixth place in the league and showed his genius for getting players to lift themselves to unexpected heights; and Brian Smith, who worked miracles at Hull, turning the drooping team of the previous year into a very sound outfit indeed.

Right
The often unsung Paul Hulme had another good game for Widnes in the championship decider against Wigan and scored between the posts putting Widnes beyond reach at 26–12.

Proof that a squad of twenty-two or twenty-three players is essential came from Castleford, who surprised everyone, not least themselves, with an outstanding first half of the season only to suffer an alarming slump. They lost their talented half-back, Shaun Irwin, and their powerful winger, David Plange, through lengthy injuries, but survived well for a time. Their Australian coach, Darryl Van De Velde, brought self-belief and discipline and a more conscientious approach to the club, and was as baffled as anyone by the late collapse. Grant Anderson, another of the club's quality youngsters, switched from centre to stand-off with some distinction and his sharp supporting play made him the club's top try-scorer. When the Test prop, Kevin Ward, was on song the pack could be awesome, particularly when the rugged Australian, Ron Gibbs, was around to add a few mean touches. Keith England and the consistent Martin Ketteridge responded well to the Aussie's presence and the skilled John Joyner enjoyed a new lease of life. The departure of Gibbs left a bigger gap than was appreciated at the time. It was also a pity that another Australian, the full-back Gary Belcher, had to leave early because of injury, for he had good attacking flair.

The Featherstone Rovers effort in finishing sixth was a magnificent performance and a great tribute to their coach, Peter Fox. Freshly promoted, Rovers did not have the money for big signings or for Australian guests, but Fox again showed his genius at getting players to lift themselves and for spotting bargains. He signed his old lieutenant, Jeff Grayshon, on a free transfer. The veteran prop, who celebrated his fortieth birthday during the season and became a grandfather, had broken his leg the previous year with Bradford Northern and had been written off. He trimmed his weight and confounded everyone, except Fox of course, by scarcely missing a match. The New Zealand hooker, Trevor Clark, who was looking for a club, was recruited and had his best season in Britain, using his pace to good effect. The loose forward, Paul Lyman, was transferred to Hull KR in exchange for the experienced second row, Chris Burton, plus cash, a deal which gave Featherstone a profit of £55,000 on transfers during the season. They leaned heavily on their half-backs, Deryck Fox and Graham Steadman. The latter benefited from the new laws giving extra space at the scrum and scored some spectacular tries, while Fox had an outstanding season, looking a superb craftsman. Featherstone also produced the season's best young find in the seventeen-year-old centre, Paul Newlove, who finished as their top try-scorer, showing a rare ability to beat opponents with pace and skill.

St Helens were an enigma. They had some dazzling moments but suffered some astonishing lapses away from home. Their Australian Test pair, the centre, Michael O'Connor, and the loose forward, Paul Vautin, were added to an already useful squad, but their league form was erratic and their best efforts were saved largely for knock-out matches. Vautin was appointed captain and led by example with some sturdy displays, while O'Connor's best was shown only in patches. Their winger, Les Quirk, showed strength and pace to collect some fine tries and the centre, Paul Loughlin, had his moments. The prop, Tony Burke, was reliable and consistent and hooker Paul Groves showed on several occasions his match-winning ability. Once the club qualified for Wembley, league form disintegrated; the seven weeks between the semi-final and

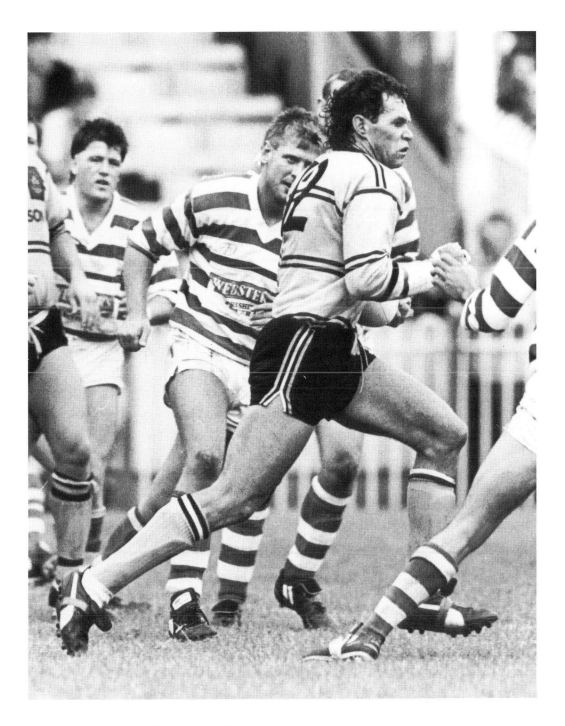

Ron Gibbs, Castleford's
rugged Australian, played an
important part in the club's
successful start to the season.
His departure for Australia left
a bigger gap than was
appreciated at the time.

That Featherstone Rovers should have finished sixth in the championship table was a magnificent effort. Their manager, Peter Fox, signed Jeff Grayshon, now over forty, on a free transfer, and Grayshon gave his coach total commitment. He trimmed his weight and confounded everyone by scarcely missing a match.

final is anyway far too long for players and supporters. However, the club snapped up two youngsters of rare promise, the full-back, Gary Connolly, and the centre, Alan Hunte, who signed as amateurs to enable them to join a BARLA Under-19 tour of Australia and are great prospects. During the week before the premiership finals St Helens showed their dissatisfaction with the team's form by putting no less than thirteen players on the transfer list and a few days later signing Jonathan Griffiths, the Llanelli RU international scrum-half, for a reported fee of £150,000.

Bradford Northern rarely realised their potential. With such as Kelvin Skerrett, Karl Fairbank, David Hobbs and Brian Noble, they had one of the most respected packs in the league. However, there was a marked lack of discipline on too many occasions, which brought a bad sin-bin record and proved costly to the club's results. The backs lacked all-round pace, despite the efforts of the sound Keith Mumby and not until Roger Simpson was moved inside from the wing did they really pose a threat. The centre, Steve McGowan, scored some good tries but his chances were limited.

Wakefield Trinity, with the New Zealand star, Mark Graham, and the Australian Steve Ella in their side, made an exciting start, three successive wins making them early leaders. However, Graham, troubled by injury and illness, announced his retirement and left for home and Ella, too, had injury problems.

Salford signed two Rugby Union internationals in the course of the season – Peter Williams (*left*) from Orrell and Adrian Hadley from Cardiff. Both suffered injury and the club's excellent start to the season was not maintained.

In addition, there were many other serious injuries, which combined to leave the side once more struggling against relegation. However, six victories from the last eight games ensured survival and celebrations at Belle Vue. Keith Rayne, John Glancy and John Thompson did sterling work up front, with Thompson switching to hooker with great success after an injury to Billy Conway, whose lively work had meant so much to the team. The return of Tracey Lazenby after a long break from the game proved a valuable move and his switch to stand-off was a winner. Trinity, too, came up with a fine prospect in Andy Wilson, a strong and speedy runner at wing or centre.

Salford were another side to begin well, but faded after the turn of the year, when their poor away form almost proved fatal. There were some good performances in the first half of the season, but injuries, notably to Peter Williams, didn't help and the departure to Australia of their sprightly stand-

David Bishop was another recruit from Rugby Union, joining Hull Kingston Rovers from Pontypool at the beginning of the season. Bishop, too, suffered injury and found it difficult to make any real impact in a side that struggled and failed to avoid relegation.

off, Paul Shaw, was clearly felt. Steve Gibson was again in fine form at full-back, Steve Kerry looked a useful recruit from Rugby Union and the centre, Ian Bragger, signed from Keighley, looked very sharp, scoring fourteen tries to finish level with Keith Bentley.

Warrington had high hopes of their 'mean machine' pack, which included the powerful Australians, Steve Roach and Les Davidson. Their clever utility back, Phil Blake, showed up well on occasions, despite having to play in various positions as injuries took their toll. Davidson had some good moments, but not enough, and not until the Challenge Cup semi-final against Wigan did Wilderspool fans really see what Roach could do. So many injuries also meant John Woods having to constantly switch positions and their title hopes never got off the ground.

The scramble for survival ended with luck going against Oldham, Halifax and Hull Kingston Rovers. All three made signings to boost their squad, and Oldham and Halifax changed coaches, but all to no avail. Oldham paid a heavy penalty for a poor defence on their travels, and only when John Cogger was signed from Runcorn did they find a player able to take chances. Hull KR were desperate to stay up in their last season at Craven Park, but it seemed too many players had grown old together. Towards the end, when their fate was virtually sealed, they turned to youth and such as Tony Sullivan, Graham Hallas and Andy Thompson showed signs of a return to the good days of the early 1980s.

Warrington had high hopes of their pack which included the powerful Australian Steve Roach. Roach did not have a particularly good season, though he was outstanding in the Challenge Cup semi-final against Wigan. Roach was again included in the Australian squad for their tour of New Zealand in July.

Halifax had a turbulent time, stemming from their decision to release the popular Graham Eadie because they had too many overseas players on their books. There was uproar among the fans and the players seemed not to respond to the methods of their new Australian coach, Ross Strudwick. Perhaps if Eadie had left for Sydney earlier rather than staying on in Halifax for several months after being released, things might have worked out better. Transfer deals brought them Brendan Hill from Bradford Northern, and Paul

Medley and John Lyons from Leeds, the last two in exchange for Paul Dixon. However, amid all the problems the fans stayed incredibly loyal and there wasn't a league attendance of less than 6,500 at Thrum Hall all season.

It's fair to say that all three relegated sides looked too strong for second division rugby and it was no surprise to hear some clubs talking again of a two-up, two-down system.

That Leigh should run away with the second division championship was predictable enough, and they suffered only two defeats in scoring 925 points. Their full-back Chris Johnson had an excellent season, and for a while winger Barry Ledger matched Martin Offiah in the try charts. Their hooker, Mick Dean, developed nicely and prop Tim Street, who gained Great Britain Under-21 honours, showed he could be a bargain signing from Wigan, if he could curb his temper.

Barrow's performance in finishing second was a triumph for their Australian coach, Rod Reddy, who had stayed in Britain during the previous summer to work with the young players at the club. His work was reflected in the team's attitude to defence, which was outstanding in the first half of the season. The scrum-half and goal-kicker, Dean Marwood, looked a splendid find and there was strong work up front from the Australian prop, Cavill Heugh, who used the experience he had gained at Halifax three seasons back to very good effect. It was no surprise when the Barrow directors persuaded Reddy to stay for another season.

Everyone in the game was pleased that Sheffield Eagles clinched the third promotion spot, a marvellous tribute to team boss, Gary Hetherington, who has worked so hard in establishing the club. He had support from a quality captain in Darryl Powell, who clearly benefited from playing first-grade rugby in the Sydney League and shattered the club's try-scoring record. Mark Aston went through the season having played and scored in every match, and there was a shrewd late-season signing for the back row in Sonny Nickle, from Hunslet, for £20,000. The one irritant for everyone at this ambitious south Yorkshire club was that while there was plenty of interest in the game shown around the area, people were still reluctant to turn up for matches. Hopefully the first division will provide an incentive, for much groundwork has been done by the Eagles in schools in the area. York and Swinton never quite found the consistency to snatch promotion, and Doncaster, whose attendances regularly topped 2,000, faded after looking well set.

Despite the glamour among the top clubs, life in the second division is never easy and ground safety regulations continue to hit many clubs hard, causing some stands to be closed. Dewsbury lost their stand in a fire and it says much for the game and the club that supporters stayed with them despite the complete lack of cover. At one stage Dewsbury had to remind spectators: 'If it looks like rain, please bring an umbrella.' A nice lesson in how to laugh in a crisis. Huddersfield changed hands and the new owners promptly changed back the name of the ground from the awful Arena 84 to that of Fartown, to general acclaim. Batley, too, changed hands and their coach, Paul Daley, overcame many difficulties to lift the club eight places during the season. Many clubs in the lower bracket would agree that while it may not be glory, that was progress.

One familiar name and a refreshing new one emerged triumphant from another great day in the Stones Bitter Premiership finals at Manchester United's Old Trafford ground. The old hands were, of course, Widnes, who won the Premiership Trophy for the fifth time with another display of solid professionalism, allied to pace and chance-taking. The newcomers were Sheffield, who added the second-division Premiership Trophy to promotion and went a long way to establishing the code in this fringe area of Rugby League territory. A crowd of 40,194 paid record receipts of £262,629, and provided a marvellous atmosphere on another notable occasion for Rugby League.

The first round produced two away victories as St Helens won at Wigan before a crowd of 18,262 and Featherstone Rovers maintained their excellent late run with a 15–12 win at Leeds. Not surprisingly, Wigan and Saints lacked a number of stars just six days before Wembley, but the Knowsley Road side's triumph was a welcome boost after their poor league run. Their unlikely hero was the prop, Paul Forber, who landed two penalty goals, his first of the season, in a 4–2 success. Steve Hampson landed one for Wigan, but failed with two late efforts which would have brought either victory or a draw which would certainly have sent League officials into hysterics. Featherstone were well led by Deryck Fox, who scored a try and landed two goals against an out-of-touch Leeds, who looked as though they might sneak it until Rovers' substitute, Glen Booth, scored the winning try four minutes from the end.

Widnes and Hull left no doubts with convincing wins. Widnes, aware of the danger from the Bradford Northern pack, once more used the pace of Martin Offiah to spearhead a 30–18 victory with a hat-trick of tries. Karl Fairbank scored one of Northern's four tries to finish the season as the club's leading scorer with twenty. Hull overwhelmed Castleford 32–6 at the Boulevard to end the Wheldon Road club's season on a depressing note after promising so much. Castleford had their full-back, Mark Gibson, sent off after fourteen minutes, though he was later found not guilty. But they already trailed 0–10 and Hull went on to collect six tries, centre Richard Price scoring twice.

Three of the second-division matches went as expected with comfortable wins for Barrow (30–5 over Whitehaven), Leigh (38–12 against Keighley) and Sheffield by 28–10 against their neighbours, Doncaster.

The exception was York's dour 4–4 draw with Swinton, which was played at Castleford because York had already moved from Wigginton Road in readiness for their new home. The replay was almost as close. Each side scored three tries, John Myler collecting his first two for Swinton, but a drop-goal by Steve O'Neill proved vital. The York player-coach, Gary Stephens, crossed in the dying seconds and everything hinged on the kick by Graham Sullivan but it was wide and Swinton were home 17–16.

Considerable interest was generated by the semi-finals, the fans wondering whether the Saints coach, Alex Murphy, could lift his team the week after their Wembley hiding. A trip to Widnes is never a rest cure, but Saints didn't let Murphy down and after a determined first-half showing trailed only 8–12 at the interval. Richard Eyres and Rick Thackray had crossed for Widnes, while Dwyer had scored the Saints try. The Widnes wings settled things in the second half. Thackray went in again, this time from sixty yards, and Offiah scored twice. Two minutes from the end he might have had a third, but was tripped by David Tanner, who was sent off. Mike O'Neill and Darren Wright also scored tries for Widnes and Jonathan Davies landed five goals to complete a 38–14 win. Mark Bailey scored the second Saints try and Tanner landed three goals, in a game watched by 12,483.

There were 11,128 at the Boulevard to see Hull destroy Featherstone Rovers 23–0 in the other semi-final. Rovers were overwhelmed as Hull, brilliantly inspired by Gary Pearce, had one of their best games of the season. Pearce scored the first try, created the second for the substitute, Rob Nolan, with an inch-perfect kick, and landed five goals and a drop-goal. Hull's other try came from the full-back, Paul Fletcher, a reward for a fine show of enterprising running. Only Chris Bibb, with a couple of long breaks, made any impact for Rovers.

The second-division semi-finals were both upsets. Swinton showed an abundance of spirit and determination to win 20–8 at Leigh, while Sheffield battled to a 9–6 success at Barrow. Swinton owed much to a tremendous display from the second row Gary Ainsworth, who scored two tries. O'Neill also scored a try and landed his customary drop-goal and there were three goals from Paul Topping. Leigh, caught napping if not fast asleep, had tries by Barry Ledger and Tony Cottrell but it was the first time the second division champions had failed to reach the final.

Barrow started well with a try by Paul Carey and goal by Dean Marwood after only five minutes, but then it became a close affair, with scrum-half Mark Aston dictating for Sheffield with splendid tactical kicking. Aston landed a penalty in the second half and Sheffield's persistence paid off when Mark Fleming scored between the posts eight minutes from time. Aston added the goal and a last-minute drop-goal to put Eagles into their first final.

Old Trafford,
Manchester,
14 May

The Second Division Premiership Trophy Final
Sheffield Eagles 43 Swinton 18

It was the greatest day in Sheffield's short history and the big crowd acknowledged the fact. Swinton were in the hunt for fifty-one minutes, but then the strain of losing their prop Steve O'Neill, sent off for a trip in the thirty-second minute, proved too much. The Sheffield scrum-half, Mark Aston, took the man-of-the-match award for his 19 points, overshadowing the hat-trick of tries by skipper Darryl Powell. It meant Aston had played and scored in every match for the club during the season and he finished as the League's leading scorer with 307. Aston also had a sizeable part in three other tries and helped rally the Eagles after a nervous start, despite his early drop-goal.

Indeed, to begin with Swinton looked much the sharper side and O'Neill's break and smart inside pass sent Alex Melling between the posts. Myler added the goal and a penalty and the Lions seemed well on top. Sheffield slowly began to find their touch and after twenty-nine minutes Aston's clever kick enabled Powell to dive in for their first try. They came again with a neat move, stopped only by O'Neill's trip on Andy Dickinson. The prop was dismissed and Aston

28

Darryl Powell holds high the second division Premiership Trophy after Sheffield's greatest day in their short Rugby League history. Their win, and promotion to the first division, was a marvellous tribute to the Eagles' coach, Gary Hetherington, who has worked so hard to establish the club. Powell proved a quality captain and had clearly benefited from playing first-grade rugby in the Sydney League the previous summer.

kicked the resulting penalty. Sheffield's renewed confidence was shown in a good try just before the interval. Mark Gamson, who was always dangerous, came on another strong run and slipped an inside pass to Aston, who sent Mick Cook over. Aston's goal made it 13–8 to Sheffield at the break.

Sheffield Eagles' captain, Darryl Powell, scored a hat-trick of tries in the second division Premiership final. Here he sprints for the line to put the match beyond Swinton's grasp. Powell shared his club's try-scoring record with 28 tries during the season.

To their credit Swinton responded with a fine move early in the second half with Mark Viller and Tony Hewitt sending their best player, Tommy Frodsham, over. Myler's goal nudged Swinton ahead again, but almost immediately Aston landed a penalty to make it 15–14 to the Eagles. They then took a decisive grip on the game with two well-worked tries inside six minutes. A dummy by the Australian Warren Smiles ended with substitute Paul McDermott scoring between the posts before Smiles and Aston combined for Powell to score. Aston added both goals and at 27–14 the game was all over.

Sheffield rammed home their advantage with further tries by Aston, Paul Broadbent and Powell, and Aston took his goal tally to eight. Swinton's only reply was Frodsham's long pass to send Scott Ranson in at the corner. Sheffield's share of the receipts and prize money came to more than £30,000. The Eagles certainly had landed.

Sheffield Eagles: Gamson; Cartwright, Dickinson, Powell, Young; Aston, Close; Broadbent, Cook, Van Bellen, Nickle, Fleming, Smiles

Substitutes: McDermott for Fleming after 20 minutes, Evans for Close after 37 minutes, Fleming returned for Van Bellen after 61 minutes, Van Bellen returned for Nickle after 64 minutes

Scorers: tries – Powell (3), Cook, McDermott, Aston, Broadbent; goals – Aston (7); drop-goal – Aston

Swinton: Topping; Ranson, Viller, Snape, Bate; Frodsham, Hewitt; Mooney, Melling, O'Neill, Ainsworth, Allen, Myler

Substitutes: Maloney for Viller after 56 minutes, Horrocks for Allen after 72 minutes

Scorers: tries – Melling, Frodsham, Ranson; goals – Myler (3)

Referee: M. R. Whitfield (Widnes)

Old Trafford, Manchester, 14 May

The Stones Bitter Premiership Final
Widnes 18 Hull 10

Pace was again the name of the game as Widnes overcame a determined Hull challenge to record a second successive League and Premiership double. Hull had some good moments, but simply couldn't match three outstanding tries from Darren Wright, Andy Currier and Martin Offiah. Currier's try was crucial. It came two minutes before the interval when Hull led 8–6 and Widnes's frustration was beginning to show. His ninety-yard touchline sprint broke Humberside hearts and swung the match. Alan Tait took the Harry Sunderland Trophy for the game's best player, a reward for some inspired running out of defence and a few important tackles.

Tait made the first clean break from Phil Windley's kick and had he seen Jonathan Davies haring up inside, there would have been a spectacular early try. A score wasn't long delayed, however. Emosi Koloto drove in on half-way and sent a masterly pass to get Wright into his stride, and Wright swept away for a fifty-yard try, Davies adding the goal. Hull were not discouraged by this set-back and good play close to the line saw Gary Divorty make the break and Paul Welham scored the try. Gary Pearce added the goal.

Both sides had their chances in a typically hard and fast game. Tait came into the line again, but Currier was held. Then Hull gave O'Hara room, but he failed to see support inside. Finally Pearce landed a penalty to put Hull ahead; it was no more than they deserved as their tackling put Widnes out of their stride. Hull then moved into a promising position for a drop-goal attempt by Pearce, but the ball was switched the other way to Richard Price on the outside. Price tried a short kick ahead but the ball was taken by Currier, who hit his stride immediately and left Pearce and Paul Fletcher treading water for a remarkable try.

That was the breathing space Widnes needed. They led 10–8 at the interval and almost immediately on the resumption won a scrum against the head on the Hull '25'. Tony Myler, who was now at stand-off for the injured David Hulme, held the ball long enough for Offiah to come ghosting inside. The winger took the pass and showed his remarkable acceleration to outpace the cover and score his sixtieth try of the season. Davies added a superb goal.

Widnes dominated play for some time after that but had to settle for a penalty goal by Davies, although Offiah thought he had scored again from a marvellous overhead pass from Myler, which was ruled forward. Hull came back with great spirit and Welham was held just short before O'Hara dived for the corner only to be ruled touch-in-goal. A television replay suggested he had scored, but referees don't have television. The only further score was a penalty by Pearce. Widnes, the professionals, had done it again.

Hull put up a magnificent fight in the Premiership Trophy final before Widnes ran out winners of yet another trophy. Paul Fletcher played steadily throughout the season and in the final his tackling often put Widnes out of their stride.

The crucial try in Widnes's 18–10 victory over Hull in the Premiership Trophy final was scored by Andy Currier just two minutes before the interval. Currier intercepted a short kick ahead by Price, hit his stride immediately and left the Hull defence treading water during a ninety-yard sprint for the line.

All Hull's supporters thought Dane O'Hara had scored when he dived for the corner in the closing minutes of the Premiership Trophy final only to be ruled touch-in-goal.

Gary Divorty was another Hull player who came back into the limelight with some excellent performances in the championship and in the Premiership. It was Divorty's break which led to Paul Welham's try in the first half and saw Hull leading 8–6 at the interval.

Widnes: Tait; Davies, Currier, Wright, Offiah; David Hulme, Paul Hulme; Sorensen, McKenzie, Grima, Koloto, O'Neill, Eyres

Substitutes: Myler for David Hulme after 39 minutes, Pyke for Currier after 49 minutes

Scorers: tries – Wright, Currier, Offiah; goals – Davies (3)

Hull: Fletcher; Eastwood, Blacker, Price, O'Hara; Pearce, Windley; Dannatt, Jackson, Crooks, Welham, Sharp, Divorty

Substitutes: Nolan for Windley after 19 minutes, Windley returned for Nolan after 40 minutes, Wilby for Price after 56 minutes, Nolan returned for Divorty after 67 minutes

Scorers: try – Welham; goals – Pearce (2)

Referee: J. Holdsworth (Kippax)

Attendance: 40,194

Hull's Welsh stand-off, Gary Pearce, was one of the key men in the club's spectacular rise up the table, his goal and tactical kicking being absolutely first-rate.

TWO

The Silk Cut Challenge Cup and the John Player Special Trophy

Paul Wilson

THE SILK CUT CHALLENGE CUP

Wembley 1989 was an event of global significance for a small corner of what used to be south-west Lancashire, and Wigan's 27–0 drubbing of St Helens will be remembered in both towns for a very long time, albeit for different reasons. The rest of the world often feels excluded when these ancient rivals meet, especially in a Challenge Cup final, and there were those who complained that St Helens's failure to give the holders a game made the Wembley showpiece too one-sided to be memorable.

This view, though understandable, takes no account of a quite superb performance by Wigan, the first team to retain the trophy on two occasions at Wembley, or of history, which suggested that St Helens, successful against Wigan at Wembley in 1961 and 1966, the only previous Cup final meetings of the clubs, bore a charmed life against their oldest adversaries.

Saints were never expected to reach Wembley in 1989, and exhibited a flicker of Cup-winning form only in the one match that mattered. An unexpected semi-final success over Widnes, the team most neutrals wanted to reach the final and perhaps the only side capable of worrying Wigan at Wembley, put Saints back in the headlines and had newspaper writers dusting off all the old clichés about Alex Murphy's Wembley 'magic'.

Murphy, as a player, had figured prominently in the two Saints wins over Wigan in the 1960s, earning some opprobrium for his blatant gamesmanship in 1966, and as player-coach had guided Leigh and Warrington to Wembley success in the early 1970s. Now he was making an eighth visit to the stadium, a record sixth in a coaching capacity, though a statistic less frequently mentioned was that on his last three visits, the ones without any playing involvement, he had returned home a loser. That record was extended to four by the events of 29 April, and Murphy, the custodian of St Helens's unbeaten tradition, returned home with his credibility, and his reputation as a Wembley magician, in tatters.

Graham Lowe, coach of the jubilant Wigan side, paid Murphy a compliment after the game by saying he was 'still a great coach of a great team', though there was precious little to support either of these claims during the eighty minutes of the final. Saints began badly and somehow managed to get worse. Their supporters had nothing whatsoever to cheer about from the moment Gary Connolly, a 17-year-old full-back cruelly exposed on his biggest day, knocked on in the first minute and allowed Wigan to set up their first try.

Making twenty-seven handling errors, missing tackles all over the pitch and looking clueless in attack, Saints became the first team for thirty-eight years to fail to score at Wembley, only the fourth in history, and possibly put up the most dismally inept performance in the history of Challenge Cup finals. Wigan, by contrast, were almost perfect. Ellery Hanley played the game of his life to collect deservedly the Lance Todd Trophy, despite strong competition from Kevin Iro, unlucky to miss out again after scoring two tries for a second year in succession. Shaun Edwards, Andy Gregory, Steve Hampson and Andy Platt were all eye-catching in Wigan's disciplined yet dashing display, in which the forwards mowed down anything above grass height and the backs – and Hanley – darted purposefully through the numerous holes made in the St Helens defence.

'They made a lot of mistakes, but we forced them into errors,' was Lowe's summary. 'We took hold of the game in the first minute and never let it go. It was as professional a performance as I have seen; we just didn't give St Helens a chance to play. I don't think many teams would have beaten us out there, you know. That was the culmination of many months of hard work, and when we get it exactly right like that, somebody suffers.'

Neither Wigan nor Saints were involved in the preliminary round, though Thatto Heath, the St Helens amateur club, won a place in the first round proper with an 18–11 success at Barrow Island, the round's only all-amateur tie. The other two amateur clubs in the preliminary round fared badly against second-division sides. Milford, of Leeds, were deprived of the right to meet St Helens in the first round when they were beaten 0–36 by Swinton; while West Hull were thrashed 2–48 by a Doncaster side determined to see Tatters Field filled for the visit of Wigan.

Hunslet and Bramley, two professional sides from the city of Leeds, failed to make the first round, the former losing 6–32 at Headingley in a derby tie against Leeds, inspired by Andrew Ettingshausen; the latter making a closer game of it at Belle Vue but still bowing out 10–18 to Wakefield Trinity. In the sixth preliminary tie, York were far too strong for Workington Town, winning 35–8.

The biggest crowd of the first round proper was at York City's football ground, where 11,347 watched Leeds, again indebted to Ettingshausen, who scored two tries and picked up a second man-of-the-match award, see off a spirited York challenge to record a 28–9 victory. There would certainly have been larger crowds at Doncaster and Salford, where Wigan and Widnes were the respective visitors, but Tatters Field was at capacity at 5000 and safety considerations limited the attendance at the Willows to 7100.

Jonathan Davies, playing only his second game for Widnes, was the chief cause of the crush at Salford, though he only came on as substitute fifteen minutes from the end. The Welshman was not sufficiently involved in the game for curious spectators to form an opinion, though Doug Laughton showed considerable confidence in his newest and rawest recruit by sending him on with the match delicately poised at 12–10 and Salford threatening to take the lead.

In the event, an Alan Tait try two minutes after Davies's entrance sealed victory for the Cheshire side, but the final score was only 18–14 and Widnes had several anxious moments on their line in the closing stages. Salford were left kicking themselves at the end for the couple of clumsy defensive errors which had presented Widnes with two of their tries. 'It was a match we could have won,' said Kevin Ashcroft, their coach. 'But we didn't realise it until too late.'

Doncaster, enjoying their biggest match for years, held Wigan to 6–8 at half-time, but once Andy Gregory came on for the visitors the Cup-holders pulled away to a 38–6 success, Joe Lydon running in four tries to claim the man-of-the-match award. Probably the toughest match of the round was the televised one, a close but compelling 7–4 victory for Castleford at Hull. Shane Horo scored the only try of the game, but the contest of two sides with Australian coaches was made memorable by the determination of both packs, and the quality of both defences. Ron Gibbs and Kevin Ward were outstanding in the Castleford pack, and afterwards Brian Smith, the losing coach, lavished praise on the victors. 'The result was close, but Cas' were the better side by a long way,' he said. 'I was proud of our efforts, but we were only engaged in damage limitation. They were calling the shots.'

Elsewhere, an out-of-sorts St Helens side recovered from a 0–4 deficit to win 16–5 at Station Road, and at the Chiswick Polytechnic ground, a hat-trick by Steve McGowan helped Bradford Northern overcome a plucky Fulham fightback in a 28–10 success. The only shock of the round came at Sheffield, where a late try by Paul Okesene brought the Eagles a 23–17 victory over Leigh, but there were some gallant failures in other ties. Rochdale Hornets made Hull Kingston Rovers work very hard indeed for their 28–24 win at Spotland: the home side led 17–6 at the interval and claimed that refereeing decisions had cost them tries and a second-round place as Rovers staged their late recovery. Thatto Heath were not disgraced at Chorley, losing only 4–8.

Paul Newlove, the young winger tipped for a great future, scored twice in Featherstone's 32–0 win at Whitehaven, but the other Cumbrian clubs fared better, Barrow beating Huddersfield 38–6 and Carlisle scoring a half century against Mansfield in a bad-tempered game which contained three dismissals.

There were no fairy tales this season for Halifax, last year's losing finalists, who were soundly beaten at Warrington; and no John Player-type ignominy for Runcorn, who lost respectably enough to Keighley. John Cogger, Runcorn's Australian loose forward, won the man-of-the-match award in that 10–28 defeat in what proved to be one of his last games for the club. Oldham, the team he was later to join, made the second round with a 40–9 win at Dewsbury.

The tie of the second round fairly leapt out of the bag. Castleford, league leaders and impressive first-round victors, were drawn at home to Widnes, the team everyone wanted to watch. Over 10,000 spectators and a sense of eager anticipation filled Wheldon Road on the Saturday afternoon in February when the teams met, but a blistering opening quarter by the visitors left the home fans, and the players for that matter, beaten and bewildered. Widnes absorbed a couple of minutes of intense pressure on their own line, then took the game into the Castleford half and struck four times in quick succession. By the time the game was twenty minutes old Tait, Emosi Koloto, Phil McKenzie and Joe Grima had crossed the home line and Castleford, unrecognisable as the defensive stonewall of the previous round, trailed 0–22.

It was a position from which there was no way back, and though Gibbs and Ward played superbly to put some pride back into Castleford, who to their immense credit managed to rally and score 18 points, Widnes pushed on with further tries from Martin Offiah and Koloto for an utterly convincing 32–18 victory.

In the other matches, Wigan, conspicuously without the unsettled Andy Gregory, scored three tries to none in a 17–4 win at Bradford; while St Helens made hard work of beating Barrow at home. The eventual scoreline, 28–6, was flattering enough, but the home fans were not impressed, and Alex Murphy employed considerable understatement when he commented after the match that the win had left room for improvement.

John Bentley, the former Rugby Union international on the Leeds wing, scored half his side's points in a 24–4 win over Carlisle, who were anything but the soft touch many had predicted; while Graham Steadman, that most under-rated of stand-offs, scored all but one of Featherstone's points in their impressive 10–4 victory at Wakefield.

Warrington, again inspired by their Australians, crushed Keighley 56–7 at Wilderspool; their veteran stand-off, John Woods, switched to the centre and collected the man-of-the-match award for scoring two tries and six goals.

Sheffield's dreams of glory were put into perspective by Oldham, though the second-division side gave a good account of themselves in a 20–32 defeat. Chorley's hopes ended in a 4–28 defeat at Hull KR, where Paul Lyman, a recent signing from Featherstone, was voted man-of-the-match for Hull KR.

The quarter-finals were once again dominated by Widnes, who attracted a lock-out crowd of 26,282 to Headingley for their pairing with Leeds. The Cheshire side were less than thrilled about being drawn away a third time, and were genuinely wary of the potential of Malcolm Reilly's expensively as-sembled side, but in the event the tie was a re-run of the Castleford game. Leeds had their moments, notably when Lee Crooks scored a try and Phil Ford brought off a magnificent cover tackle on the speeding Offiah, but they had no answer to the speed of Widnes's thought and movement.

Just as they had done at Wheldon Road, Widnes seized control with three tries in a short period in the first half, all from forwards. Richard Eyres, the eventual man-of-the-match, opened the scoring, and Grima twice finished off slick handling moves before the interval. Leeds rallied in the second half, but any thoughts of a revival after Crooks's try were dampened by the emergence of Kurt Sorensen, whose inclusion on the substitutes' bench had meant a seat in the stand for Jonathan Davies. With their Kiwi captain and packleader on for Derek Pyke, Widnes made the final score 24–4 with tries from Andy Currier and Offiah, though the winning margin could easily have been greater had the former managed more than two goals from six attempts, or the latter accepted a couple of inviting try chances.

It was a bad day all round for Yorkshire. Featherstone and Hull KR, the White Rose's remaining representatives in the competition, went out to St Helens and Warrington respectively. Neil Holding, coming on as substitute, collected the 100th try of his career and inspired Saints to a 32–3 success at Knowsley Road, while at Craven Park, Phil Blake was outstanding in Warring-ton's 30–4 win in his last game before returning to Australia.

The fourth quarter-final brought together Oldham and Wigan at a snow-covered Watersheddings. With their shock Cup exit on the same ground in 1987 always at the back of their minds, Wigan had to work hard for a 12–6 win, and only made the game safe late in the second half with a try by Kevin Iro.

Central Park,
Wigan,
11 March

The Challenge Cup Semi-final
St Helens 16 Widnes 14

Widnes, after their compelling performances in previous rounds, were the side everyone wanted to avoid in the semi-finals, and St Helens, whose progress to the same stage had been anything but impressive, were widely felt to have drawn the short straw for a thrashing. St Helens seemed to have nothing in their favour, especially when Manly refused to allow Michael O'Connor and Paul Vautin to appear in the game, though they did have Murphy, a coach with a gift for exploiting apparently hopeless situations.

Murphy had been hard at work during the week before the game, making what capital he could out of the few Widnes weak points. They were making a big mistake by not playing Davies, he said, and were in danger of believing their own publicity and thinking they only had to turn up at Central Park to get to Wembley.

It is impossible to say whether the pre-match bluster from Knowsley Road had any bearing on the outcome of the semi-final, though events did more or less conform to Murphy's predictions. Widnes, in the face of nothing more than honest endeavour and sheer determination from St Helens, never settled into their stride, never seized control of the game as they had done at Castleford and Leeds, and were beaten by Les Quirk's second try three minutes from the end.

Of course there was rather more to it than that. The post-mortems, especially those conducted by the Widnes contingent, centred on the fate which befell Richard Eyres in the nineteenth minute. The Widnes loose forward and main playmaker tripped Holding, and in accordance with the controller of refereeing's new directive received instant dismissal. The consensus at the ground was that Eyres's reflex action would have been more appropriately punished by a spell in the sin bin, but Fred Lindop's decree had removed the referee's discretionary powers, and John Holdsworth had no option but to point to the tunnel.

Having to play an hour of a semi-final with only twelve men was hard on Widnes, especially as they held a lead before Quirk's late clincher, but even before Eyres departed there was evidence that Saints had the edge on the favourites. Quirk's opening try was just one of several chances the underdogs created, and though Widnes hit back with tries by Darren Wright and David Hulme, they were caught again just before the interval when Darren Bloor crossed by the posts.

Widnes claimed that the match turned on the dismissal of Eyres, though St Helens, with some justification, could say the crucial moment was a copy-book cover-tackle on Offiah by Gary Connolly, the 17-year-old amateur full-back. Either way, the semi-final was a treat to watch for the neutral spectator: eighty minutes of pulsating action, with the underdogs winning through a try in the closing minutes, represented everything a cup-tie should be.

Gary Connolly, the seventeen-year-old St Helens full-back, was cruelly exposed on his biggest day after playing an outstanding game for St Helens in the semi-final of the Challenge Cup against Widnes.

St Helens: Connolly; Tanner, Veivers, Loughlin, Quirk; Holding, Bloor; Burke, Groves, Forber, Haggerty, Harrison, Cooper

Substitutes: Jones for Forber after 54 minutes; Bailey not used

Scorers: tries – Quirk (2), Bloor; goals – Loughlin (2)

Widnes: Tait; Thackray, Currier, Wright, Offiah; David Hulme, Paul Hulme; Grima, McKenzie, Pyke, Mike O'Neill, Koloto, Eyres

Substitutes: Sorensen for Pyke after 51 minutes; Dowd for Currier after 76 minutes

Scorers: tries – Wright, David Hulme; goals – Currier (3).

Referee: J. Holdsworth (Leeds)

Attendance: 23,119

Maine Road, Manchester, 25 March

The Challenge Cup Semi-final
Warrington 6 Wigan 13

If St Helens were thought to have drawn the more difficult semi-final opponents, Wigan, it appeared, had the easier task. Warrington had not had the best of seasons, flirting with relegation in the league and only accounting for lesser sides en route to Maine Road.

Graham Lowe was quick to challenge the dangerous assumption that the semi-final would be a walkover for his Wigan team. 'People are talking as if we were at Wembley already, but I did not feel relieved when we drew Warrington,' he said. 'In the last few years we have been beating Widnes and Saints on a regular basis, but in the time I've been at Wigan I think Warrington have beaten us more times than we've beaten them.'

Lowe's caution was well founded, for like all Warrington and Wigan meetings, the second semi-final was hard fought and desperately close. Warrington, who had flown Steve Roach back from Australia for the game, played with a resolve which belied their lowly league status, and were nearer to matching Wigan than the scoreline suggests. A late try by Shaun Edwards, goaled by Lydon, gave the holders a flattering margin of victory, but what really took Wigan to Wembley was an astonishing 61-yard drop-goal by Lydon which broke a 6–6 stalemate eight minutes from time.

Until that moment Warrington had looked capable of forcing a replay at least. They had achieved their stated intention of preventing Wigan scoring tries from their own half, but had understandably overlooked the possibility of drop-goals from beyond the half-way line. Lydon's monstrous kick dominated discussion of the match as completely as the Eyres incident had done in the earlier semi-final. 'I just hit it and hoped', said Lydon afterwards, with unconvincing modesty. 'I was going to kick for touch but someone shouted go for goal, and I thought what the hell.'

Lydon's effort was worth only a single point, but Warrington heads dropped, along with several thousand lower jaws, when the ball bisected the uprights, and Edwards's late try, from Ellery Hanley's kick, was mere decoration. The drop-goal alone would perhaps have earned Lydon the man-of-the-match award, but he had also scored a try in the first half and two goals in the second, so his case was unanswerable.

This was harsh on John Woods, who in attempting to reach Wembley at the thirteenth attempt had been Warrington's most creative and dangerous player. His three penalties brought Warrington their points, and his brilliant break almost brought a decisive try for Tony Thorniley, only for Steve Hampson and Tony Iro to stop the young winger a yard short of the line.

There were bruises in both dressing-rooms afterwards, and both sides acknowledged the efforts made by the other. It was left to Maurice Lindsay, the winning chairman, to stress the significance of Wigan's achievement. 'Everyone knows that St Helens and Wigan have only met at Wembley twice, and that Wigan were humiliated on both occasions,' he said. 'There are fervent supporters in Wigan who feel that nothing this club has achieved is of any significance until Saints have been beaten at Wembley. The odds against both clubs making it to the final in the same year are very long, so I'm delighted to have the chance to set the record straight.'

Warrington: Lyon; Drummond, Cullen, Darbyshire, Thorniley; Turner, Woods; Roach, Roskell, Boyd, Thomas, McGinty, Mike Gregory

Substitutes: Duane for Mike Gregory at half-time, Richards for Cullen after 78 minutes

Scorer: goals – Woods (3)

Steve Hampson appeared in a
Wembley final at last after missing
Wigan's three previous visits through
injury. It was Hampson who started
the move which led to Kevin Iro's
third-minute try.

Wigan: Hampson; Tony Iro, Kevin Iro, Lydon, Bell; Edwards, Andy Gregory; Lucas, Kiss, Shelford, Potter, Platt, Hanley

Substitutes: Betts for Lucas after 16 minutes; Goodway for Potter after 48 minutes

Scorers: tries – Lydon, Edwards; goals – Lydon (2); drop-goal – Lydon

Referee: M. R. Whitfield (Widnes)

Attendance: 26,529

Wembley
Stadium,
29 April

The Challenge Cup Final
St Helens 0 Wigan 27

'It looks like Wigan have got a bye at Wembley,' was the terse reaction of a Widnes fan, as his side inflicted the heaviest home league defeat since the war on St Helens, just sixteen days after their semi-final encounter. The disenchanted voice from the stand probably did not know how right he was.

St Helens, by Murphy's own admission, played 'like statues' at Wembley. Wigan, to be fair, would have given most other teams a similar mauling, but with a proud record and the town's self-esteem at stake, Saints completely failed their faithful supporters. Long and loud were the recriminations afterwards, with whole pages of letters in the local press, and the common themes were a sense of betrayal, and the pain which Saints, not Wigan, had inflicted on their followers at Wembley.

Eight miles away it was carnival time. Wigan, relieved to find that 1961 and 1966 were just defeats, and not manifestations of some cosmic principle, celebrated in style. T-shirts bearing the simple slogan '27–0' appeared on the streets; the score, as Andy Gregory had pointed out after the game, expressed everything. 'I looked up at the scoreboard just before leaving the pitch, because I wanted to treasure the memory,' the scrum-half said. 'It seemed too good to be true, even then. It felt good to win so well, but maybe it will take a while for our performance to get the credit it deserves.'

Gregory, winner of the Lance Todd Trophy a year earlier, was pipped on this occasion by Hanley, whose colossal impact on the final began in the second minute when after a period of pressure, occasioned by Connolly's nervous first fumble, Saints had to drop out from their own line. Steve Hampson, appearing in a Wembley final at last after missing three previous Wigan visits through injury, fielded the ball casually on half way, and handed on to Hanley, who powered deep into the Saints left flank. Easily avoiding an ineffective challenge from Roy Haggerty, the Wigan captain drew the cover and slipped out a pass to Kevin Iro, who was able to hold off Paul Loughlin and crash through Connolly and Tony Burke on the line. Wigan's first-ever try against St Helens at Wembley had taken just three minutes to arrive, and the pattern for the final was already set: missed tackles and dropped balls on the Saints side, powerful running and clinical finishing from Wigan.

It was Wigan's tenacious tackling, however, which dominated the next twenty minutes. St Helens, ominously disorganised at this early stage, could make no headway down the middle and seemed incapable of moving the ball to the wings. The only opportunities which came their way were not even half

43

chances – a run down the centre from Shane Cooper after a short ball from Haggerty, and a glimmer of an opening for O'Connor on the right from which the winger unwisely elected to kick – but on both occasions, Saints were not only halted but dispossessed.

Andy Gregory, who had a fine game, celebrates another Wigan try. 27–0! 'I looked up at the scoreboard before leaving the pitch: it seemed too good to be true', he said.

Kevin Iro scored Wigan's first try in only the third minute of the final, crossing the line after crashing through Connolly and Tony Burke amid a flurry of falling bodies.

Lydon scored his first goal with a sixteenth-minute penalty, but the try which confirmed Wigan's superiority, sealed the man-of-the-match award for Hanley, and will haunt St Helens for many years to come, arrived in the twenty-fifth minute. Receiving the ball a couple of yards inside his own half, Hanley exploded again into the Saints defence, this time going all the way. Vautin was effortlessly wrongfooted and left floundering, then as a quartet of defenders converged on the loose forward twenty yards from the line, Hanley found extra speed and strength to burst out of custody, and half stride, half stumble his way to a touchdown by the posts.

Lydon's second goal gave Wigan a 12–0 interval lead, but within five minutes of the restart Gregory dropped a highly significant goal, one which obliged Saints to score at least three times. There was nothing to suggest that Saints were capable of scoring at all, however, as more passes went to ground and the final became a personal nightmare for Haggerty, the most frequent offender.

Wigan showed how to string a series of passes together in the forty-eighth minute, when Platt, Hampson and Dean Bell transferred the ball crisply to the right wing, where Kevin Iro again had the strength to disdain the option of passing outside and reached the line through despairing challenges from Connolly and Cooper.

In the sixty-fifth minute Edwards tricked the hapless Haggerty to break clear from half-way and set up the next try, sending the supporting Gregory over from close range when Edwards was halted by a good cover tackle from Paul Groves. With Holding, Groves was one of the few St Helens players to emerge with credit from the final, though Connolly did something to restore his reputation when he pulled down Lydon on the left wing.

Wigan were not to be kept out for long, however, and five minutes from the end an expert series of long passes, almost nonchalantly executed by Edwards, Bell and Gregory, transferred the ball from the right wing to the left, where Lydon gave Hampson a generous overlap for the full-back to score a popular try.

Murphy's response to the embarrassing failure was predictable and rather lame. 'We need six new players,' he said. 'Wigan were in a class of their own out there. We were armed with pea-shooters, and they had cannon.' All true, possibly, but the coach needed to accept at least a portion of the blame for his initial selections, his failure to make changes quickly enough when things started to go wrong on the pitch, and the complete absence of any moves or tactical awareness in the St Helens display.

Lowe, undecided about his future in England after completing his three-year contract at Wigan, could afford to deflect attention onto his players as the tributes arrived thick and fast. An emotional person at the best of times, Lowe was moved to tears when 30,000 people turned up to welcome the Cup-winners back to Central Park. 'Thank you for letting me be your coach,' he told the gathering. 'Wigan have the best players and supporters in the world.' Lindsay, his chairman, was more specific and more contentious. 'Wigan now have the best collection of talented players ever assembled at a Rugby League club,' he said. Older generations of Central Park supporters might take issue with that, but for once no one in St Helens had the stomach for an argument.

Shaun Edwards was another who played outstandingly well in Wigan's disciplined yet dashing display in the final at Wembley.

Ellery Hanley, the outstanding player of the season, and the first British player to win the Golden Boot award, enjoyed a truly remarkable Challenge Cup final. Hanley played the game of his life in that match and deservedly picked up the Lance Todd Trophy.

St Helens: Connolly; O'Connor, Veivers, Loughlin, Quirk; Cooper, Holding; Burke, Groves, Forber, Dwyer, Haggerty, Vautin

Substitutes: Evans for Dwyer after 46 minutes; Bloor for Loughlin after 64 minutes; Dwyer returned for Haggerty after 67 minutes

Wigan: Hampson; Tony Iro, Kevin Iro, Bell, Lydon; Edwards, Gregory; Lucas, Kiss, Shelford, Platt, Potter, Hanley

Substitutes: Goodway for Potter after 67 minutes; Betts for Kiss after 72 minutes

Scorers: tries – Kevin Iro (2), Hanley, Gregory, Hampson; goals – Lydon (3); drop-goal – Gregory

Referee: R. Tennant (Castleford)

Attendance: 78,000 (capacity)

The 1988–89 John Player Special Trophy final – the last, as it happened, under that name – was overshadowed to a large extent by the arrival of a slight, nervous young man from Wales. Jonathan Davies, a Widnes player for just under two days, watched from the Burnden Park stand as his new colleagues took on Wigan, attracting more media attention than the game itself.

The ballyhoo surrounding Davies's decision to turn professional robbed Wigan of the limelight they deserved after beating a strongly-fancied Widnes side to lift the JPS Trophy for the third time in four years. Davies's popularity had aligned most neutrals to the Widnes cause; everyone, it seemed, wanted to see Doug Laughton's enterprise in assembling a fast and exciting side rewarded; but the fairy-tale was not to be. Laughton, in fact, was to admit later that the timing of the Davies signing had been a handicap to Widnes.

'With hindsight, I think it might have been better to have kept quiet about Davies until after the final,' the Widnes coach said. 'The whole thing came at the wrong time, really; I was down in Wales when I should have been helping the lads prepare, and all the fuss in the media did not help our concentration. 'The timing was unavoidable though, because we wanted Davies before the Challenge Cup deadline, and he couldn't have pulled out of the Welsh training squad without giving the game away. It was a pity the two events clashed, but we got ourselves a great player, even if it did cost us the competition.'

Widnes's interest in the captain of Wales had surfaced a week or so earlier, and prior to gaining his signature, Laughton had mischievously included Davies as substitute in his final line-up. The deal, variously reported as being worth between £150,000 and £250,000, was struck in Wales on the Thursday before the final, but by Saturday Laughton had changed his mind about putting Davies straight into the team. The pressure of making a début in a televised final would have been too much, he reasoned.

Wigan, meanwhile, had been following events with a mixture of envy and curiosity. Unused to being kept out of the headlines by other clubs, or going into finals as underdogs, Wigan wondered, like the rest of Rugby League, where Davies was going to fit into the talented Widnes side. Wigan themselves kept an unusually low profile as they approached the final, though a *frisson* of excitement had been generated at Central Park by a sequence of events involving Andy Gregory, the club's international scrum-half and a former Widnes player, who had been dropped following a surprise transfer request. Conveniently, Gregory patched up his quarrel with Graham Lowe, Wigan's New Zealand coach, in time to be named as substitute for the final, and ended up supplying the pass for Ellery Hanley's winning try.

The 12–6 scoreline belied Wigan's superiority; in a defence-dominated game Widnes might not have scored at all had not Adrian Shelford presented Darren Wright with an interception try. 'I think Widnes might have been victims of their own publicity,' said Maurice Lindsay, the Wigan chairman, after the game. 'All we've heard this week is what a great team Jonathan Davies has joined. People tended to forget that Wigan are a great team too.'

Two Wigan teams went into the bag for the first round of the competition, St Patrick's, the local amateurs, having disposed of Elland to proceed from the preliminary round with Bramley, Featherstone and Castleford. Their fates could hardly have been more different. St Pat's were drawn away to Sheffield Eagles, where the gulf between second division and amateur standards was underlined by an emphatic 80–8 home victory, while Wigan were drawn away to Runcorn Highfield in a tie destined for notoriety. Runcorn switched the game to Central Park but, saddled with a players' strike, could only field a team of mainly local amateurs, and were thrashed 2–92. That was bad enough, but the back pages on Monday morning also featured Bill Ashurst, their coach, in action on his less than auspicious return to the scene of his former playing glory. Ashurst, 41, had gone on to make up the numbers, but lasted only minutes before being dismissed for a blatant head-butt on Andy Goodway. A repentant Ashurst later offered his resignation. 'I let the club down as well as myself,' he said. 'I was provoked, but as a born-again Christian I don't think I should have done what I did.'

Four first-division clubs went out at the first round stage, Salford, Oldham and Featherstone losing away to Halifax, Warrington and Widnes respectively, and Leeds surprisingly stumbling at home to Castleford. The last tie, an eagerly awaited confrontation between the Yorkshire Cup finalists, produced another thrilling game and a vintage performance from Gary Belcher, the Castleford full-back, though Leeds were unhappy about an alleged trip on Garry Schofield by Bob Beardmore. Malcolm Reilly, the losing coach, said the scrum-half's action had cost his side a certain try, and should have been punished by dismissal.

Castleford, undefeated at the top of the first division under Darryl Van De Velde, their new Australian coach, entered the second round with confidence, but were brought quickly down to earth by Bradford Northern, who travelled to Wheldon Road and won by a single point. A David Hobbs drop-goal provided the vital margin in a 19–18 win, though Northern had scored three tries, through Johnson, Pinner and Fairbank, to Castleford's two.

Wigan were run close by Halifax at Central Park, where only a late individual try by Mark Preston prevented a replay. Halifax had led 14–10 at half-time, but second-half tries by Joe Lydon and Preston brought Wigan a 20–16 win. Widnes's 32–9 win at Sheffield was comfortable enough, though it was Paul Okesene of the Eagles who won the man-of-the-match award. Hull Kingston Rovers, however, were glad of a hat-trick by Chris Close, their Australian centre, to see off a spirited Chorley Borough revival at a sticky Victory Park.

Barrie Ledger scored three tries in Leigh's 40–8 rout of Doncaster, while Les Quirk, his replacement on the St Helens wing, claimed a touchdown in a hard fought 16–13 victory over fast improving Hull. Wakefield Trinity and Warrington both ran in seven tries against second-division opposition, Rochdale and Bramley being on the receiving end. Leigh, the only second-division representatives left by the quarter-final stage, put up a tremendous performance at Odsal to hold Bradford for most of the game, finally capitulating to a try and a goal from Hobbs in the second half.

St Helens gave their supporters a scare by allowing Wakefield to run up an 18–2 lead after twenty-two minutes of the game at Knowsley Road, but the holders steadied to 14–18 by half-time, and eventually ran out 34–18 winners, Paul Vautin scoring a try and taking the man-of-the-match honours. Widnes also trailed at half-time in their derby with Warrington, but an opportunist try from Martin Offiah cancelled Les Davidson's opening effort, and inspired by Phil McKenzie and Kurt Sorensen, the Chemics scored twice more for a 16–7 victory.

Tony Iro is well and truly tackled in the John Player Cup final against Widnes which Wigan won 12–6.

Wigan had threatened to draw 16–16 in the second round and managed it at Hull KR in the quarter-final, squandering a 12–8 interval lead through uncharacteristic lapses of concentration in defence. David Bishop was narrowly wide with a last minute drop attempt which could have won the game for Rovers, but, like Gavin Miller, was unavailable through injury for the replay. Lacking their two main inspirations, Rovers were a pale shadow of their real selves three days later at Central Park, losing 0–30.

The first semi-final paired Widnes and St Helens at Wigan, and was closer than many had predicted, the Cheshire side winning an exciting game by 20–18. Refusing to be overawed by their opponents' reputation, Saints tackled with relentless determination, and though they were caught once in the first half by the sheer pace of Offiah, they led 8–4 at the interval through a Les Quirk try and two Paul Loughlin goals. Offiah struck again when Tony Myler shrewdly kicked deep to catch Phil Veivers out of position, but Saints countered with Quirk's second, from a splendid run by Michael O'Connor. The holders looked home and dry, but Widnes stuck at their task professionally, brought on Derek Pyke for Joe Grima, and carried the game back to Saints. The defensive concentration which had been so impressive earlier suddenly evaporated, and alarming gaps began to appear in the Knowsley Road side's rearguard. Andy Currier strolled between transfixed defenders for the try which brought Widnes back into the game, and a couple of minutes later Richard Eyres administered the killer blow after Alan Tait had taken the ball deep into the danger area. Laughton was magnanimous in victory. 'We didn't deserve it,' he said.

Joe Grima was one of the rocks on which Widnes's success was built during the season. He had a great game in the John Player semi-final against St Helens, which Widnes surprisingly lost; in the quarter-final against Leeds Grima twice finished off slick handling moves before the interval.

The second semi-final brought Wigan and Bradford together at Headingley. Wigan went into the game as favourites and by virtue of scoring three tries to none emerged as clear victors, though the struggle was far harder than the 16–5 scoreline might suggest. Bradford, an unfashionable side with a not wholly undeserved reputation for dour play, contributed much to an entertaining afternoon, but some of their good work was undone by some petulant remarks afterwards by Barry Seabourne, their coach.

Seabourne saw fit to criticise David Carter, the referee, for his handling of the game, an outburst which eventually cost him a £250 fine. It was hard to understand the coach's complaint. True, Wigan scored two crucial tries through Lydon and Tony Iro while Brian Noble was in the sin-bin late in the second half, but there was no arguing that the hooker had tripped Tony Iro, and many referees, including Fred Lindop, the new controller, would have dismissed Noble for good. Similarly, Pinner was lucky to escape with a sin-bin sentence for an obvious swipe at Hanley, Wigan's first-half scorer. The indiscipline appeared to be all on the Bradford side, especially when the dissent by Paul Harkin which gave Wigan a further two points was taken into consideration, plus the fact that Brendan Hill missed the match through suspension. Seabourne possibly realised that Bradford's own misdemeanours had played a significant part in their downfall, but in seeking to transfer the blame onto the referee he merely highlighted his players' shortcomings, and reflected little credit on himself.

Burnden Park,
Bolton,
7 January

The John Player Special Trophy Final
Widnes 6 Wigan 12

Most of the outside broadcast equipment in the north of England turned up at Bolton to record the meeting of Wigan and Jonathan Davies's 'new team', even though the former Wales captain's involvement in the day's events was limited to blinking under the television lights at an impromptu press conference, chatting to a BBC interviewer on the pitch, and waving to his new fans from his seat in the stand.

Davies's arrival had put the spotlight on the other Union converts in the Widnes side, however, and to a man they failed to respond. Tait, whose consistency at full-back had brought him to the brink of international recognition, succumbed to nerves and lost his personal battle with Wigan's Steve Hampson. Offiah, the speed merchant on the left flank, was starved of the ball and well policed on the few occasions he threatened. And Emosi Koloto, the big Tongan in the pack who had made giant strides in his first season in British Rugby League, had to be substituted shortly after the interval after conceding two disastrous penalties, both kicked expertly by Lydon.

The massive interest in Davies had concealed other Widnes weaknesses too. Sorensen, their Kiwi skipper, was clearly not fit, and his inspiration was sorely missed. Myler, at stand-off, was all too easily dominated by the quicker, more alert Shaun Edwards. For a team which had promised so much, Widnes were a disappointment. Wigan, the side everyone had been prepared to write off, proved their doubters wrong in the most convincing way possible.

An Edwards kick, misjudged by Tait, almost resulted in a try for Hanley in the opening exchanges, but the referee ruled that the ball had not been properly grounded. Undeterred, Edwards, who was revelling in the scrum-half role that Gregory's relegation to the bench had thrust upon him, played a significant part in Wigan's first try after just six minutes. Responding quickly to take the ball from Sorensen, Edwards ran straight at the heart of the Widnes defence, then, as the cover closed in, slipped Ged Byrne into the gap he had created on the right. Byrne continued the attack intelligently, running straight for the corner flag but unloading a crisp reverse pass at the right moment for Kevin Iro, coming in from the wing to work the scissors, to force himself through Mike O'Neill's tackle on the line.

Lydon missed the goal, but such an early try was ominous for Widnes, especially as they continued to handle nervously and exhibit basic communication breakdowns in defence and attack. Clearly the Cheshire side were having an off day, but it was greatly to their credit that they never allowed Wigan to run away with the final.

The Widnes tackling, at least, was an area of their game which remained up to its usual standard, though it is debatable whether they would ever have taken the lead had not Shelford made Wright a gift of a try in the thirteenth minute. The big Kiwi prop was one of Wigan's best performers on the day, despite having to leave the field mid-way through the first half for attention to a head wound, but when he received the ball in the right centre's position on the half-way line, he appeared perplexed what to do next. After carefully looking round he elected to throw an ambitious ball to the wing, but only succeeded in finding Wright, that persistent infiltrator of opposing threequarter lines, who caught the ball cleanly and beat off Lydon's despairing chase in a fifty-yard run to the posts.

Andy Currier's straightforward goal gave Widnes a lead they scarcely deserved, but they surrendered the advantage six minutes later when Koloto occasioned Shelford's temporary withdrawal with a rash challenge, and Lydon thumped over the penalty from forty yards.

The teams remained level at 6–6 until the interval, but a couple of minutes into the second half Koloto committed his second indiscretion, an unnecessary and rather obvious lunge at Dean Bell. As Lydon accepted another long-range penalty to put Wigan back in the lead, Laughton brought off his disappointed Tongan for the more experienced Paul Hulme.

Widnes hearts sank further when Gregory joined the fray in the forty-eighth minute, replacing the limping Lydon, though Lydon himself had returned by the time Hanley scored his decisive try twelve minutes from the end. Gregory, with a neat pass round Joe Grima, was involved in the move, but the Wigan captain took his opportunity with customary panache, moving to the right and accelerating past Offiah and David Hulme.

Smug smiles abounded in the winners' dressing-room afterwards. 'We all wish Jonathan Davies the very best, but now he will know that Widnes are not the only team with great players,' said Lindsay. 'People seemed to forget that Ellery Hanley, Dean Bell, Steve Hampson, Andy Goodway, Andy Gregory, Joe Lydon and the Iro brothers are all great players too.' Davies, for his part, parried questions gracefully and diplomatically. Yes, he could see that Wigan were the better team on the day, and no, he didn't imagine Widnes played like that all the time. A Rugby League player for a matter of hours, Davies was asked what he thought of his first game. 'Is it always that hard?' he replied.

Widnes: Tait; Thackray, Currier, Wright, Offiah; Tony Myler, David Hulme; Sorensen, McKenzie, Grima, Mike O'Neill, Koloto, Eyres

Substitutes: Paul Hulme for Koloto after 43 minutes; Dowd not used

Scorers: try – Wright; goal – Currier

Wigan: Hampson; Bell, Kevin Iro, Lydon, Tony Iro; Byrne, Edwards; Shelford, Dermott, Wane, Betts, Potter, Hanley

Substitutes: Goodway for Shelford after 20 minutes, Shelford returned for Potter after 32 minutes, Gregory for Lydon after 48 minutes, Lydon returned for Byrne after 64 minutes

Scorers: tries – Kevin Iro, Hanley; goals – Lydon (2)

Referee: J. Holdsworth (Leeds)

Attendance: 20,709

Mark Preston, a convert from Fylde Rugby Union who had won an England B cap, played some good games on the wing for Wigan when the Iros or Bell were unavailable. He was in the championship decider against Widnes and played for Lancashire in the War of the Roses match before going off injured at half-time.

THREE

The Grünhalle Lager Lancashire Cup, The John Smith's Yorkshire Cup and the Rodstock War of the Roses match

John Huxley

THE GRÜNHALLE LAGER LANCASHIRE CUP

The more cosmopolitan of the two county competitions in professional Rugby League retains its popularity even under pressure from the bigger tournaments. That point was emphasised when the attendance figure at only one of the first round matches, and that an outpost game between Carlisle and Chorley Borough, failed to top the 1000 mark.

Indeed, little Runcorn, who nestle on the Cheshire bank of the Mersey just a stone's throw from Widnes, must have been smiling contentedly because the pain of a 4–42 trouncing by another of their first-division neighbours, Warrington, was considerably eased by a gate return of 4500. Barrow, coached by the former Australian Test forward, Rod Reddy, had begun their run to promotion from the second division and gave the Cup-holders, Wigan, a good game in front of 5528 people, eventually going down by 10–24. At Naughton Park the league champions, Widnes, had 10,714 packed into their stadium for their meeting with St Helens.

The Saints followers must have thought that they had wasted both time and money as the Chemics raced into a 22–0 half-time lead. However, the second period was more rewarding as Alex Murphy's team put the brakes on Widnes; St Helens must have regretted that first-half collapse as they were just short, at 24–32, when the final hooter went.

Oldham ran away with their tie, hammering a Workington Town team led by the former Great Britain coach, Maurice Bamford, 64–2, and Salford, producing some of their most stylish and fluid football, ended Whitehaven's interest with a 42–8 romp at the Willows. In a meeting of two leading second-division clubs, Swinton beat Leigh 24–14 but that proved just a hiccup for the Hilton Park club on their way to promotion and the divisional title.

One of the key aspects of any knockout tournament is the provision for the Davids to smite the Goliaths. Alas, there was to be no romance in the second round of the Lancashire Cup. Rochdale Hornets, spending their first season sharing the Spotland Stadium with their impoverished Football League fourth-division soccer neighbours, and still awaiting the outcome of a multi-million pound sale of their Athletic Ground headquarters, faced Wigan at Central Park. A 36–4 win for Wigan did nothing to suggest that the gap between the first and second divisions is closing though the result at Wilder-

54

spool, where Carlisle went down 18–34 to Warrington after a spirited fight, was more reassuring. Meanwhile Salford and Widnes gained the other two semi-final placings with respective wins over Oldham and Swinton.

In modern Rugby League the demands on the top players, especially the overseas recruits, can conflict. For the Widnes and Wigan contingents in particular the semi-final was almost an embarrassment. The two clubs were due to meet on 5 October but because Wigan had three players, Kevin and Tony Iro and Dean Bell, involved in the World Cup final in New Zealand five days later they sought Widnes's agreement to delay the game by a week. Widnes, who also had their prop, Kurt Sorensen, involved with the Kiwi team, were happy to acquiesce. Whether they would have agreed so readily after the game is debatable.

Sorensen never made it back from New Zealand for the re-arranged tie, much to Widnes's muted anger, while for Wigan Kevin Iro was ruled out through injury. However, both Bell and Tony Iro played as Wigan gained a 14–10 victory and a fifth successive place in the final. To a large extent Wigan's win was made possible because Sean Tyrer, the replacement for their full-back, Steve Hampson, whose leg injury from the earlier victory over Barrow persisted, landed five goals. This must have been a source of both pleasure and pain to his father Colin, a former Wigan full-back star himself but that night an assistant coach to Doug Laughton at Widnes.

A week earlier Salford had reached their first county final since 1975–76 by beating Warrington. The game was made memorable for the Red Devils when their expensive wing signing from Welsh Rugby Union, Adrian Hadley, landed three vital goals. Salford, who had spent the two previous seasons fighting against relegation, were riding high in the Stones Bitter Championship and their arrival in a competition final was greeted with almost universal delight throughout Rugby League. Warrington, understandably, were among the exceptions.

Knowsley Road, **The Lancashire Cup Final**
St Helens, **Wigan 22 Salford 17**
23 October

After the trauma of the early season injuries and the loss of their New Zealand stars on World Cup duty, Wigan walked into their fifth successive final in a confident frame of mind. The record book was in their favour. It was the fourth successive time that the final had taken place at Knowsley Road, St Helens; it was Wigan's thirty-fourth appearance at this level in the tournament; they were looking for their twentieth final win and their fourth successive victory. Salford, on the other hand, were making their first appearance for fourteen years and seeking their first win since 1972–73. The odds were not helped by the fact that while Wigan had been market leaders for some years Salford had struggled to keep their first-division life since being promoted in 1984–85.

Nevertheless Salford approached the game in a confident frame of mind. Their irrepressible coach, Kevin Ashcroft, tried hard to convince anybody who would listen that Wigan were not unbeatable. He said: 'We are not going to Knowsley Road to lose!' But weighing against the Salford chances was the suspension of their unorthodox Australian full-back, Steve Gibson, who had been sent off against Oldham a week earlier. His appeal against a two-match ban had failed just days before the final and Salford were forced to switch Peter Williams, their recruit from Orrell Rugby Union, into the no. 1 jersey, with their goal-kicker, Ken Jones, moved into the centre berth.

Salford's New Zealand international prop forward, Peter Brown, missed a penalty in the first minute of the match but he did succeed in hitting the target in the twenty-third minute with a penalty after the Wigan full-back, Steve Hampson, had been sent to the sin-bin for a less than elegant tackle on Salford's Australian stand-off, Paul Shaw. Seven minutes later they built further on the lead with a Mick Worrall drop-goal but then the fact that Salford had been able to resist for such a length of time finally brought a response from Wigan.

Paul Shaw, Salford's Australian quicksilver stand-off, flanked by Adrian Shelford of Wigan in the Lancashire Cup final, won by Wigan 22–17.

The dexterity of Wigan's scrum-half, Andy Gregory, created a gap which Kevin Iro exploited with the game's first try in the thirty-fourth minute and he added the conversion. The impressive New Zealander was back on target again three minutes later when he flighted an accurate penalty after Mick Worrall had been penalised for a high tackle on Shaun Edwards.

If Wigan had thought that might crush Salford's resistance, they were wrong because ten minutes into the second half the underdogs created a four-man move which ended with the winger, Tex Evans, going in for a try. Brown's goal-kick bounced back off the upright. A penalty for offside five minutes later gave the big Kiwi a chance to atone and his successful kick left Salford trailing at 8–9. However, Wigan were well equipped to deal with such pressure and a three-try burst took them well clear.

In the sixty-seventh minute Gregory sent the New Zealand prop, Adrian Shelford, who was playing on the ground where he might have been a player, in for a try. Then Salford suffered a major loss when Williams had to be taken off with concussion and they were still reshuffling their forces when Wigan's Salford-born forward, Denis Betts, put Kevin Iro in for his second try in the sixty-ninth minute. The match seemed to have reached a conclusion seven minutes from the end when Jones failed to control a high kick from Edwards and Ellery Hanley's tackle sent the ball stuttering across the goal-line for another of Wigan's New Zealand contingent, their centre Dean Bell, to touch down. Kevin Iro, who had missed with conversion efforts after the two previous tries, added the goal points.

However, Salford were not ready to concede the game. In the seventy-seventh minute Brown created a gap for his centre, Keith Bentley, to score a try and as the game moved into injury time the New Zealander assisted in a move that saw one of his fellow forwards, Steve Herbert, go in for a try. Unfortunately for Salford, Brown's goal-kicking prowess deserted him on the day and he missed both conversions, leaving him with a return of two successes from seven attempts. The fact that Salford lost by only 17–22 emphasised Brown's lack of accuracy and consistency.

Wigan: Hampson; Tony Iro, Kevin Iro, Bell, Lydon; Edwards, Gregory; Lucas, Dermott, Shelford, Platt, Goodway, Hanley

Substitutes: Betts for Lucas after 49 minutes, Byrne for Lydon after 76 minutes

Scorers: tries – Kevin Iro (2), Shelford, Bell; goals – Kevin Iro (3)

Salford: Williams; Evans, Bentley, Jones, Hadley; Shaw, Cairns; Herbert, Moran, Brown, Gormley, Worrall, Horo

Substitutes: Blease for Williams after 68 minutes, McTigue for Horo after 74 minutes

Scorers: tries – Evans, Bentley, Herbert; goals – Brown (2).

Referee: K. Allatt (Southport)

Attendance: 19,167

THE JOHN SMITH'S YORKSHIRE CUP

Huddersfield have twenty Yorkshire Cup final appearances to their name though the last time they got to the final was as far back as 1960–61. Now a second-division side, this once great name of Rugby League is a mere ghost of its former self and their first-round humiliation, a 12–94 defeat at Castleford, brought little joy to anybody including the victorious home club. In fact, Darryl Van De Velde, Castleford's Australian coach in his first season in Britain, said: 'It was embarrassing to see a professional club with so little ability, and I felt for my players as they had to keep heaping further agony on a team that should not have been on the same paddock'.

Three Castleford players, Chris Chapman, David Plange and Kevin Beardmore, each collected a hat-trick of tries while the second-row forward, Martin Ketteridge, landed thirteen goals. The only consolation on offer to the Huddersfield fans, those few that remain, was that that result was a major factor in a change of management later in the season, which at least hints at a much needed revival.

The size of entry to the White Rose county's competition means that there has to be a preliminary round involving two ties. Leeds claimed their place in the first round proper by beating their second-division neighbours, Bramley, 36–14 while Wakefield Trinity clipped the wings of Sheffield Eagles in a comfortable 28–6 win.

Signs that Hull KR's season was heading for trouble were clearly visible when they came close to grief in a 28–22 win at second-division Keighley. At half-time, the Humberside club were leading comfortably 18–4 but they found Keighley considerably more difficult to handle in the second period, running out only narrow winners.

Hull, on the other hand, had few problems as they demolished Hunslet 53–0. Four of their players, Dane O'Hara, Gary Divorty, David Moon and Paul Eastwood, each scored two tries while Eastwood landed six goals.

In an evenly matched tie Leeds overcame Bradford Northern 24–21 at Headingley in front of the round's biggest crowd of 10,950. Northern had their chance to make it into the second-round draw when they led 17–8 at the interval. However, coach Malcolm Reilly's half-time pep talk must have struck the right note as Leeds fought back with conviction in the second half. With four tries apiece it came down to goal-kicking, David Stephenson's four for Leeds against two by David Hobbs and a Paul Harkin drop-goal for Northern. That defeat put the Cup-holders out of the competition. Featherstone Rovers, who had left the second division at the start of the season, comfortably accounted for Doncaster 38–8 while Halifax put the worries of a poor start to the season firmly behind them as they cruised to a 36–14 win over Batley with their Australian full-back, Graham Eadie, later to leave Thrum Hall in strained circumstances, landing four goals.

Wakefield Trinity, another of the promoted clubs, had little trouble in dealing with their second-division neighbours, Dewsbury, winning 46–20 with their Australian import, Steve Ella, kicking seven goals and their winger, Phil Fox, crossing for a hat-trick of tries.

York made it to the second round after beating Mansfield Marksman 25–4, and they were the only second-division club to survive the first round. It was their misfortune to be drawn against Castleford, who at that stage of the season were running into one of their finest veins of form for several years. The north Yorkshire side could not resist and they were beaten 14–40 as Castleford, the previous season's beaten finalists, moved into the semi-finals.

Of the remaining ties Leeds had the toughest assignment as they faced one of their oldest rivals, Wakefield Trinity. Another big crowd of 11,150 was attracted to Headingley and they saw a tight encounter. Trinity were still in contention at 6–6 at half-time but goal-kicking proved their undoing as Andy Fletcher landed just two for Wakefield while Garry Schofield had one of his rare moments in the role of goal-kicker for Leeds to land three. Leeds's scrum-half, Ray Ashton, also hit the mark with a drop-goal.

Halifax comfortably accounted for Hull KR 24–2. The Humbersiders folded after a sustained first-half effort when they restricted the previous season's Challenge Cup finalists to a 4–0 lead. The overall result was to be a rare moment of joy for the Thrum Hall club who had to face relegation at the end of the season. However, Humberside hopes remained high as Hull put up a stout defence to stop Featherstone Rovers from scoring as they moved through to the last four by winning 18–0. All the scoring came in the first half and then it was simply a case of Rovers running up against a proverbial brick wall.

That left four well matched teams – Castleford, Halifax, Hull and Leeds – in the competition. Coincidentally or otherwise, three of them were in the charge of Australian coaches, Darryl Van De Velde (Castleford), Ross Strudwick (Halifax) and Brian Smith (Hull), all of whom were in their first season with a British club. Malcolm Reilly, the sole remaining British coach, who doubled as Great Britain's national team coach, led Leeds to play the rapidly emerging Hull while Halifax and Castleford faced each other at Thrum Hall.

The coincidences did not finish there either, because both semi-finals were settled with 12–8 scorelines. It was one of the rare games when Leeds's Australian import, the Test prop forward, Sam Backo, had any real influence on the result. Backo scored one of the tries in their victory over Hull while Castleford made sure of a place in the final by resisting a strong attempt by Halifax. A try by the former Test centre, Tony Marchant, settled the issue.

Elland Road, Leeds, 16 October

The Yorkshire Cup Final
Leeds 33 Castleford 12

Both protagonists share a reputation for providing fast, open football in almost direct contrast to what is expected from two Yorkshire clubs, where forward play is the norm and less adventurous tactics are the rule rather than the exception.

Leeds were establishing a new record of twenty-one county final appearances, moving ahead of the ill-fated Huddersfield. Their arrival at Elland Road at least signified that the ambition they had displayed by investing so much money in transfer deals was beginning to yield the kind of reward they were seeking. Castleford, on the other hand, three-times winners of the Cup since 1977–78, were establishing themselves as possible championship contenders by leading a highly competitive Stones Bitter Championship table.

The possibility of a notable final had attracted a crowd of 23,000 and they were not to be disappointed. Neither team was prepared to compromise its principles and attack was very much the order of the day. In fact, Castleford were the first to pay the price for adhering too closely to those principles because, after four minutes, a pass from the Castleford stand-off, Grant Anderson, was intercepted by the master of the half-chance, Garry Schofield, and the try was predictable.

The initial shock of that early reverse was mollified for Castleford when the second row, Martin Ketteridge, who must surely be within range of the Great Britain team, kicked a penalty only to have the score cancelled almost immediately when Leeds's other Great Britain centre, David Stephenson, kicked a penalty and Schofield edged over a drop-goal. There was no doubting Castleford's courage as they kept driving forward and they registered their first try when their centre, Giles Boothroyd, swept in to touch down after a build-up by Anderson, their Test winger David Plange, and the Australian full-back Gary Belcher.

Lee Crooks and Colin Maskill hold high the Yorkshire Cup after Leeds had beaten Castleford 24–14 in the final at Elland Road, Leeds.

Castleford's desire to keep pushing forward left them defensively stretched. In the twenty-sixth minute the Leeds forward, Lee Crooks, exploited a defensive blunder to link with his full-back, Gary Spencer, to create a second try for Schofield. The Wheldon Road team reduced the Leeds advantage five minutes later when their loose forward, John Joyner, swapped passes with Plange to score in the corner and Ketteridge landed a superb goal from the touchline.

Leeds's control of the match extended into the second half when Stephenson kept up their momentum with a penalty but the real damage to Castleford's aspirations came in the fifty-second and fifty-eighth minutes. Each time the Leeds winger, Carl Gibson, was the man to deliver the *coup de grâce*. The first blow came when Joyner's pass on the sixth tackle to substitute David Roockley, deep in the Leeds half, was intercepted by Gibson who raced eighty yards

for the try. Gibson's second strike was the final nail in Castleford's coffin. Stephenson was the architect of the move and Gibson the executioner. A Stephenson conversion saw Leeds move very quickly from their half-time lead of 15–12 to 27–12 and from that point the match was settled. Substitute Paul Medley, whom later in the season Leeds were to transfer to Halifax, swept in for a try in the sixty-seventh minute and in the last minute Stephenson landed a penalty which gave him a record six goals for the Yorkshire Cup final to add to his Lancashire Cup final record of six.

For Reilly, besides the satisfaction of landing his first major trophy with Leeds, there was the triumph of beating a club with whom he had a long career as both player and coach. He said: 'I am delighted for everybody at Leeds but especially for the players, who are among the best I have ever worked with.'

For Castleford it was their second successive defeat in the Yorkshire final and set the pattern for their season when they became the 'almost' men of 1988–89, providing good attractive rugby but winning nothing.

Leeds: Spencer; Ettingshausen, Schofield, Stephenson, Gibson; Lyons, Ashton; Crooks, Maskill, Waddell, Powell, Brooke-Cowden, Heron

Substitutes: Medley for Brooke-Cowden after 53 minutes, Backo for Waddell after 64 minutes, Brooke-Cowden returned for Heron after 66 minutes

61

Scorers: tries – Schofield (2), Gibson (2), Medley; goals – Stephenson (6); drop-goal – Schofield

Castleford: Belcher; Plange, Marchant, Boothroyd, Chapman; Anderson, Bob Beardmore; Ward, Kevin Beardmore, England, Ketteridge, Gibbs, Joyner

Substitutes: Roockley for Chapman after 46 minutes, Sampson for Roockley after 59 minutes, Roockley returned for Joyner after 72 minutes

Scorers: tries – Boothroyd, Joyner; goals – Ketteridge (2)

Referee: M. R. Whitfield (Widnes)

Attendance: 23,000

THE RODSTOCK WAR OF THE ROSES MATCH

In any serious war there has to be a battle, but Rugby League has managed to find a conflict where that particular method of sorting out an argument has been overlooked. Inspired by the hugely successful Australian State of Origin matches, where passions are inflamed by the meetings of New South Wales and Queensland, the British Rugby Football League decided to institute their own version between the traditional rivals Lancashire and Yorkshire.

The old county championship, which also included Cumbria, had been brought to a close in 1982–83 after it had lost its credibility as a meaningful tournament. Selections were devalued as the competition's importance declined and as spectators fell away.

Backed by sponsorship from the Wigan-based company, Rodstock Enterprises, the War of the Roses came to life in 1985. Rodstock's considerable publicity machine rolled into action and the game sat back awaiting a success. However, this annual match has failed to ignite the imagination either of the spectators or, more important, of the Lancashire players.

Lancashire went into the 1988 encounter still seeking their first win in the series; Yorkshire, inspired by their coach, Peter Fox, had won all the previous matches. For the fourth game Lancashire decided to try a new approach, introducing Widnes's Doug Laughton as coach in place of Alex Murphy from St Helens who, unusually for a man more used to success, had failed to find a winning formula in any of the previous meetings.

Under Murphy, Lancashire had never produced a team which reflected the strength of the game in their county, and Laughton was affected by the same malaise. Three international-class players, the Wigan half-back, Shaun Edwards, the Widnes centre, Darren Wright, and Warrington's loose forward, Mike Gregory, all withdrew through injury and the fragile Red Rose commitment to the fixture wilted further even before a ball had been kicked.

The War of the Roses
Yorkshire 24 Lancashire 14

Theoretically, Laughton's selection of eight Widnes players in his squad of fifteen should have given them some sort of identity but, in the first half, that did not appear to be the case. Yorkshire, well drilled and motivated, completely dominated the game. The Great Britain captain, Yorkshireman Ellery Hanley, who had just settled a contractual wrangle with his club Wigan, scored the game's first try after three minutes and the Bradford second rower, David Hobbs, converted. Henderson Gill, another Wigan-based Yorkshireman, continued to heap points on Lancashire's head with a twenty-second-minute try and then, three minutes later, Hobbs, who had missed the conversion, landed a penalty to give Yorkshire a 12–0 lead that should have been greater given their monopoly of the game.

Below
The sterling efforts of Paul Loughlin (St Helens) failed to bring victory to Lancashire in the War of the Roses match.

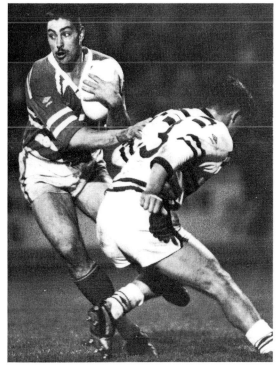

Right
The Leeds winger, Carl Gibson, who scored two tries in six minutes in the Yorkshire Cup final against Castleford, had helped Yorkshire, yet again, to win the War of the Roses match.

The first indications that Lancashire were contesting the match seriously came nine minutes into the second half when the Widnes winger, Rick Thackray, forced his way over for an unimproved try. However, a Yorkshire reply was not long in coming. Two minutes later the Castleford centre, Tony Marchant, conjured up another try which was goaled by Hobbs. Lancashire's appetite for the game returned when the Widnes pair, the centre Andy Currier,

63

and their substitute back, Barry Dowd, went in for fifty-seventh and sixty-seventh-minute tries, the latter being converted by Paul Loughlin of St Helens who had had such a successful summer tour of Australia with the Great Britain side.

The White Rose, however, came to full autumn bloom when the Leeds centre, Garry Schofield, playing in front of his home crowd, crushed Red Rose resistance with a final try in the seventy-first minute and Hobbs landed the conversion. So Peter Fox's commitment and passion for the Yorkshire cause remained the dominant feature of this series and it brought the overall tally for meetings between the two counties to forty-one each. Perhaps that will set Lancashire – and the series – alight this year.

Yorkshire: Roockley (Castleford); Gill (Wigan), Marchant (Castleford), Schofield (Leeds), Gibson (Leeds); Hanley (Wigan) Deryck Fox (Featherstone Rovers); Hobbs (Bradford Northern), Kevin Beardmore (Castleford), Kelvin Skerrett (Bradford Northern), Dixon (Halifax), Powell (Leeds), Goodway (Wigan)

Substitutes: Steadman (Featherstone Rovers) for Gill after 58 minutes, Heron (Leeds) for Skerrett after 50 minutes

Scorers: tries – Hanley, Gill, Marchant, Schofield; goals – Hobbs (4)

Lancashire: Lydon (Wigan); Thackray (Widnes), Currier (Widnes), Loughlin (St Helens), Preston (Wigan); David Hulme (Widnes), Andy Gregory (Wigan); Pyke (Widnes), Kiss (Wigan), Wane (Wigan), Mike O'Neill (Widnes), Roberts (Warrington), Paul Hulme (Widnes)

Substitutes: Dowd (Widnes) for Preston after 44 minutes, Eyres (Widnes) for Roberts after 50 minutes

Scorers: tries – Thackray, Currier, Dowd; goal – Loughlin

Referee: M. R. Whitfield (Widnes)

Attendance: 8,244

FOUR

The British Coal Nines Tournament

Ray French

When the first ever British Coal Nines tournament was held in 1987 many who were involved in its inception were well aware that the new format was a huge gamble. Players, coaches, spectators and viewers of BBC TV's *Sportsnight* programme no doubt looked for an extended version of Sevens rugby. By the end of the second British Coal Nines, held on Wednesday, 2 November at Central Park, Wigan before a 7,000 crowd, all acknowledged that the experimental nine-a-side version of Rugby League not only encouraged the open running and passing normally associated with Sevens, but demanded the strong forward play and solid defence of the full thirteen-a-side game.

The presence of two guest sides, the President's Nine, with ex-Union stars, Peter Williams and Adrian Hadley, and a Rest of the World team which included the experienced Mark Graham from New Zealand, Australia's scrum-half sensation, Allan Langer, and Papua New Guinea's centre and captain, Bal Numapo, plus the six leading first division sides, ensured three hours of thrilling entertainment.

Widnes, with exciting runners like Alan Tait, Martin Offiah and Tony Myler in their line-up, were immediately installed as favourites, with Wigan, the holders of the trophy, considered by many to be the team to trouble the Chemics. But, as always with this mini-version of League, there were plenty of shocks in a first round which highlighted the necessity of team work for success.

Both the Rest of the World side, coached by the Australian national team coach, Don Furner, and the President's Nine, with the Great Britain manager, Les Bettinson, in charge, were to struggle in the first round despite both teams being packed with international stars. The opening matches with the President's Nine against Leeds (lost 4–6) and the Rest of the World against Bradford Northern (won 4–0) proved the difficulties in assembling star players unaccustomed to each others' play. The need to field five forwards in a pack ensures that there is a considerable amount of forward play in any nine-a-side match and any successful team must have cohesion between the pack and the scrum-half, who invariably acts as the ball carrier.

Against Leeds, the President's Nine moved the ball from touchline to touchline and caused Leeds's Cliff Lyons to pull off a couple of superb cover tackles, but they lacked strength and understanding in the middle and especially in the pack. The Rest of the World side, thanks to a lone Ashley Gilbert try, struggled to beat a weak and inexperienced Bradford Northern side, and displayed a lack of overall speed which was to prove decisive at the finish.

Easily the fastest team on paper, Widnes, were expected to coast through the first round, especially when the ex-Rosslyn Park Union wing, Martin Offiah, raced round St Helens's Union recruit from Neath, Mike Carrington, to open their scoring. Tries from Carrington, gaining his revenge on Offiah with a monstrous hand-off before touching down at the corner, and their prop, Paul Forber, plus two Michael O'Connor goals, eased St Helens into a deserved lead. When Widnes's Andy Currier converted his own try just before the final whistle, the Wigan crowd, in a dilemma as to whether they should roar on their deadly rivals the Saints, or urge on the favourites Widnes, settled back for a period of extra time.

It is always heartbreaking to lose a match in extra time through a penalty goal but such was Widnes's fate when Saints' Australian Test star, Michael O'Connor, settled the issue with a well struck kick. The cheers from the crowd at the departure of St Helens from the stage soon turned to jeers as the local heroes, Wigan, bowed out, rather surprisingly, to a well balanced and determined Warrington side. Led by the hardworking forwards Mike Gregory, Mark Roberts, and Billy McGinty, the Wires soon showed robust forward play to be a vital asset in Nines rugby. Turning a 0–6 deficit into a winning 12–6 margin, Warrington's forwards supported the incisive breaks of John Woods and rocked Wigan in midfield with rugged defence. The victory smiles on the Warrington players' faces at the end of their first match were nothing to the size of the grin on the face of their coach, Tony Barrow, who maintained his record of never losing a match to Wigan at Central Park since becoming first-team coach.

Perhaps the most gripping match of the evening, between Leeds and the Rest of the World in the first semi-final, best illustrated the determination of the competing teams to win the £6,000 prize money on offer to the winners. Leeds's speedy second row, Paul Medley, highlighted the glaring defensive weaknesses of the overseas stars when he sped in for two tries, both converted by David Stephenson. But, in attack, the Rest of the World had a sufficient number of talented performers to tie the match 12–12 with a try from Mark Graham and a try and two goals from Peter Brown. For over six minutes both sides were locked in battle in the extra-time period before the Australian loose forward, Gavin Miller, settled matters for the Rest of the World with a try after one of his typical driving runs.

It was significant that the coaches of the club sides, obviously learning from the previous season's tournament, had stressed the need for defensive line-ups and had packed their sides accordingly with noted tacklers. Such was Warrington's strength and the reason they eventually emerged as winners of the tournament. Saints' coach, Alex Murphy, too had stiffened up his pack with such noted tacklers as Paul Vautin, Shane Cooper, and Paul Forber but his side finally had to concede defeat to the only try of the match when Warrington's wing, Mark Forster, took advantage of a kick ahead by the shrewd John Woods. The talented Woods converted the try to give Warrington a narrow win by 6–0.

That nil scoreline for St Helens was the forerunner of yet another pointless score from the Rest of the World, who met Warrington in the final. Warrington's extra speed in the backs, where Mark Forster with two tries and John

Woods proved outstanding, and their greater commitment in the pack proved too much for a dispirited and tiring overseas side. Brian Carbert and Mark Roberts took advantage of sensibly placed kicks upfield to take the final score to 24–0 in Warrington's favour. The Rest of the World's stars had proved a huge attraction to the crowd but their inability to train under their coach, Don Furner, for any length of time was cruelly exposed by Warrington. And it was a very tired Gavin Miller, Allan Langer and company who trooped up to the rostrum to receive the £4000 for the runners-up from Martin Cruttenden, the sales director of British Coal.

John Woods of Warrington, the winner of the man-of-the-series award in the final of the British Coal Nines, evades a despairing tackle from Arnold Krewanty while Craig Coleman, who played so well for Hull in the championship, awaits developments.

Warrington's coach, Tony Barrow, had seen his team fall at the first hurdle in the inaugural Nines tournament in 1987. For the 1988 tournament he had certainly done his homework and learned from the mistakes of the previous year. His success was founded on a solid defence which conceded only one try in forty-six minutes of high-speed, all-action play. He had realised that Nines calls for tough forward play as much as the speed of a Mark Forster or a Brian Carbert. And in John Woods and Mike Gregory Warrington possessed two players who could turn the result of a game with a blistering break, a perfectly judged pass, or a devastating tackle. To win any mini-tournament, whether it be Nines or Sevens, a team must possess a player who can dominate a match and dictate affairs in midfield. Whether plying his pack with short passes, opening out play to his backs, chip-kicking ahead of a tight defence, or breaking down that defence with a daring break, John Woods directed Warrington's affairs and fully deserved to pip his team mate, Mike Gregory, for the man-of-the-series award of a cheque for £250 and an inscribed miner's lamp.

at Central Park, Wigan, Wednesday, 9 November 1988

Leeds	President's Nine	Bradford Northern	Rest of the World
John Lyons	Andy Mason	Richard Francis	Arnold Krewanty
Norman Francis	Kevin Pape	Roger Simpson	Bal Numapo
David Stephenson	Peter Williams	Basil Ake	Steve Ella
Paul Medley	Paul Shaw	Heath Godfrey	Allan Langer
Carl Gibson	Paul Round	Steve Lidbury	Peter Brown
Cliff Lyons	Kevin Beardmore	Peter Seabourne	Gavin Miller
Ray Ashton	Colin Whitfield	Paul Rhodes	Mark Graham
Mark Brooke-Cowden	Gary Divorty	David Croft	Ron Gibbs
David Heron	Adrian Hadley	Glen Barraclough	Mark Horo
Gary Price	Keith Bentley	David Hamilton	Craig Coleman
Colin Maskill	Darryl Powell	Steve McGowan	Ashley Gilbert

St Helens	Widnes	Warrington	Wigan
Paul Loughlin	Alan Tait	David Lyon	Joe Lydon
Mike Carrington	Darren Wright	Robert Turner	Tony Iro
Michael O'Connor	Andy Currier	Mark Forster	Mark Preston
Les Quirk	Richard Eyres	Brian Carbert	Ged Byrne
Shane Cooper	Martin Offiah	John Woods	Bobby Goulding
Darren Bloor	Tony Myler	Gary Sanderson	Kevin Iro
Paul Forber	David Hulme	John Thursfield	Augustine O'Donnell
Paul Vautin	Kurt Sorensen	Mark Roberts	Ian Lucas
Shaun Allen	Phil McKenzie	Mike Gregory	Phil Clark
Phil Veivers	Emosi Koloto	Billy McGinty	Andy Goodway
David Tanner	Paul Hulme	Ron Duane	Dennis Betts

Round 1	Leeds v	6	(try – Gibson; goal – Stephenson)
	President's Nine	4	(try – Bentley)
	Bradford Northern v	0	
	Rest of the World	4	(try – Gilbert)
	St. Helens v	14	(tries – Forber, Carrington; goals – O'Connor 3)
	Widnes	12	(tries – Offiah, Currier; goals – Currier 2)
	Warrington v	12	(tries – Turner, McGinty; goals – Woods 2)
	Wigan	6	(try – Goulding; goal – Kevin Iro)
Semi-finals	Leeds v	12	(tries – Medley 2; goals – Stephenson 2)
	Rest of the World	16	(tries – Graham, Brown, Miller; goals – Brown 2)
	St Helens v	0	
	Warrington	6	(try – Forster; goal – Woods)
Final	Warrington	24	(tries – Forster 2, Carbert, Roberts; goals – Woods 4)
	v		
	Rest of the World	0	

The British Coal man-of-the-series: John Woods (Warrington)

Referees: J. Holdsworth (Kippax), R. Whitfield (Widnes)

Attendance: 7,000

Mike Gregory, a hard working
forward for Warrington throughout
the tournament, receives the British
Coal Nines Trophy from Martin
Cruttenden, British Coal's sales
director. Gregory is followed by Billy
McGinty.

FIVE

Five Players of the Season

Trevor Watson

Choosing five players of the season is perhaps the quickest way I know of losing friends, anyway for a time, but at least you don't have many people to buy drinks for.

There is great personal satisfaction this time because no overseas player has come into the group, and all five could represent Great Britain. It would be nice to think that this was a measure of the improvement of British players because clubs still imported a number of top-class men from Australia and New Zealand for the season. Obviously there were several other strong candidates for my list and, for the first time, two players have been selected from one club, and one player appears for a second successive year. One other point in favour of the chosen five is that none of them caused problems for their clubs or their coaches; and that surely is an important part of any player's make-up.

ELLERY HANLEY (WIGAN)

The 1988–89 season was the one in which Ellery Hanley underlined his value as the game's outstanding player, a fact recognised even in Australia. If anything, Hanley grew in stature during the season and with a flood of commanding all-round displays wiped out the belief that he is basically a finisher. You can't mark Hanley. His strength, speed and superb balance on those curving runs enabled him to score a number of high-quality tries, and he created many others with his ability to break the first tackle.

Hanley also came firmly into his own as a top-class defender. His strength again served him well in this respect as did his ability to read the game, which so often put him in the right spot to cover any emergencies. His tackling is often copybook and there was also a readiness to drop on the loose ball in the face of flying feet.

As a captain Hanley commanded complete respect and many feel he will develop into a top-class coach; nothing seems beyond his capabilities. He crowned an outstanding season with a superb display at Wembley. He towered over the Cup final in magnificent style and seemed able to produce something more or less at will. All this was from a player who had returned from a demanding tour the previous summer and had played in Sydney club rugby before his return home. It was little wonder the Australians were queueing for his services again.

There is no doubt that Ellery Hanley was the season's outstanding player. A magnificent performance in the Challenge Cup final, following outstanding displays in the championship and in internationals, was capped by the Golden Boot award in Australia in July.

Martin Offiah finished the season with another sixty tries, making no fewer than 100 in his first two seasons of Rugby League. For Widnes he was a matchwinner and a crowd pleaser, with an ability to score tries from anywhere.

The consistently good performances of Deryck Fox, perhaps more than any other factor, lay behind Featherstone's outstanding season. He never lacked heart and showed a readiness to take on the responsibility of organiser and tactician.

MARTIN OFFIAH (WIDNES)

It is one of the constantly amazing facts of Rugby League life that after scoring more than 100 tries in his first two seasons in the game, Martin Offiah still has to prove himself in the eyes of some followers and critics. During the season it became a game within a game to pick out Offiah's so-called failings, but wisely he ignored the criticism and continued doing the thing at which he excels – scoring tries. When all has been carefully dissected, one undoubted fact remains, that every club in the game would like to have the Widnes winger in their side because of his ability to score tries from anywhere; and there is also no doubt that his arrival would increase attendances. What more can be asked?

Offiah began his second season in Rugby League under much pressure after an astonishing first season, yet continued to score tries at an even greater rate. Some of his efforts were exceptional, including the one in the Premiership final which few, if any other, wingers could have scored. There was also one against Leeds when he sliced through the middle of the field and then ran in an arc round the full-back, Andrew Ettingshausen, himself no slouch, and beat him for speed on the outside.

Offiah finished the season, when he was very much a marked man, with sixty tries to his credit, twenty-six ahead of his nearest rival. He is a crowd pleaser and a matchwinner, and did both on many occasions.

DERYCK FOX (FEATHERSTONE ROVERS)

There was no question that the Featherstone Rovers scrum-half, Deryck Fox, was facing the most testing season of his career at the start of 1988–89. He was in a team likely to struggle and tipped by many for a quick return to the second division. Some also, quite unfairly, questioned whether Fox was good enough to perform consistently well at top club level. He answered all those questions in impressive fashion and was perhaps the main reason why Rovers had such a good season and finished so high in the table.

Fox has never lacked heart, and during 1988–89 he also proved to be a splendid craftsman and showed a readiness to take on the responsibility of organiser and tactician. He developed steadily in all those aspects in a typical no-fuss fashion and scarcely missed a game. He was very strong in possession, showed a great tactical appreciation of when to open things out and was equally ready to take on the extra burden of being the side's kicker, both out of his hands and at goal. Given Fox's usual willingness to do more than his share of work on defence, he lived up well to the reputation that Featherstone has earned over the years for producing scrum-halves of great strength, character and courage. Fox may lack that extra yard of pace, but there were precious few matches in which this showed as he again displayed the knack of bursting into space to create chances for his support players.

David Hulme,
the second
Widnes player in
this selection,
played an
important part in
keeping the
club's well oiled
machine working
smoothly
throughout the
season. He
showed an ability
to call the shots
on attack and
proved rugged on
defence.

Andy Dannatt
added speed to
his undoubted
strength and
never shirked the
demands made on
him by Hull's
new coach, Brian
Smith. Dannatt
must now have
come back into
contention for
international
honours.

DAVID HULME (WIDNES)

Among the many big names at Widnes, there was one player vital in keeping their well-oiled machine working smoothly, their half-back, David Hulme. Hulme had made his name on tour during the summer but, perhaps unfairly, was still regarded as mainly a stopper. However, 1988–89 was the season when he emerged as a planner and organiser in the best traditions.

It says much for David Hulme's all-round ability that it became difficult to pin a positional tag on him, for he was able to slot in at scrum-half and stand-off and be equally effective. Indeed, when the Chemics lost Tony Myler through injury, Hulme took on Myler's role with a rare degree of skill and composure. He showed an ability to call the shots on attack, proved rugged on defence and his touch-kicking was an additional important factor.

One of David Hulme's best performances came in defeat. He was superb as an organiser when the side were reduced to twelve men after the dismissal of Richard Eyres in the Challenge Cup semi-final. He did his job so well, even without the proper cover of a loose forward, that Widnes virtually controlled the second half and came desperately close to a remarkable victory. All this was done in completely unassuming fashion, although he took much pleasure in recording the 100th try of his career during the season. His term ended forty-two minutes early because of injury in the Premiership final, but long before then Hulme's point had been proved.

ANDY DANNATT (HULL)

Hull's re-emergence as a force to be reckoned with was based on a good deal of effort by local players and no one did better than their prop, Andy Dannatt. He has tended to fade out of things in recent seasons after looking a very fine prospect, but 1988–89 was the year when he came into his own, showing a high degree of dedication and fitness. The poor start by the team called for unstinting effort to pull things round and Dannatt took on a seemingly thankless task in good style and never shirked his responsibility.

Dannatt is certainly no lightweight, but it was impressive to see him still running with great energy in the later stages of hard matches and he appeared to have put on speed to add to his undoubted strength. In the past he has not always used his strength in the right way, but this time he knuckled down and adjusted to the demands made upon him by the new coach, Brian Smith, to become a good, hard-working front row.

It is one of the disappointments at the Boulevard that Dannatt's international career has been on hold for around four years, when a stream of representative honours were there for the taking. He has now come back into contention and in view of the importance of the visits by New Zealand and Australia in the next two years, a close eye will be kept on him. He proved he can do a fine job for club and country.

SIX

The Amateur Game

Ron Girvin

Perhaps the most important development on the amateur front during 1988–89 was the introduction of the British Coal National Youth League for amateur and professional Under-19 teams from each district, a move that ended the long-running dispute between BARLA and the Rugby Football League over Colts teams. Naturally there have been some teething problems, but generally the new set-up was a success. Indeed, the St Helens director, Bill Lyon, commented at one point: 'The whole development set-up is proving of immense benefit not only to ourselves but to the community as a whole. We are understanding and working with our amateur neighbours and there is a real feeling of common purpose as we strive to improve the participation and standards of our sport'.

In the British Coal League, the young lads from St Helens set the standard for future teams to follow. They were unbeaten in the premier division and then made it a double by winning the eight-team grand final play-off. West Hull, who finished third in the premier division, were the victims in the final at the Boulevard, going down 8–20. The Saints' scrum-half, Shaun Devine, took the man-of-the-match award for his action-packed display. In fact, he opened the scoring with a penalty, but Darren Oglesby quickly equalised. Two tries in five minutes just before half-time put Saints well on the way to the double. Their stand-off, Andrew Fairclough, made the first try for prop Peter Beckett and then the Great Britain centre, Alan Hunte, Jason Roach and the substitute Neil Gavin, combined to put Kevin O'Garra in. Devine's two goals gave Saints a very comfortable half-time lead of 14–2 and the match was virtually put beyond doubt eight minutes after the interval when Devine intercepted on the half-way line and raced away for a try which he goaled himself. Lance Cator got a late consolation try, before being sent off with Carl Cooper of St Helens, and Oglesby kicked the goal.

There could not have been a better finish to the Rodstock National League than the title being decided in the very last game at West Hull. The Humbersiders were two points behind the shock team of the season, Wigan St Patrick's, at the start of the game, but they knew that if they could win by more than a 15-point margin then they would be champions at last. In the first two seasons West Hull had been runners-up while St Patrick's had been wooden spoonists.

But that final game proved something of an anti-climax as West Hull ran out 45–0 winners to take the title. It was a scoreline no one in Lancashire could believe, but in fairness St Patrick's were without four key players and it was always going to be hard to win at Hull anyway. Ironically the game should have been the opening one of the season but West Hull had been granted an open date to play in France.

Trying to hide his disappointment, St Patrick's joint coach, Jimmy Taylor, commented: 'If someone had said to me at the start of the season that we were going to be second we would have settled for that. But after getting so close it is a bit aggravating'. To make matters worse, St Patrick's lost 0–2 in a dour National League Cup final to Egremont at Hilton Park, Leigh. The vital penalty-goal came from John Brocklehurst, although the Cumbrians twice got to the line but could not get the ball down.

Wigan St Patrick's had promised better things at the end of the previous season, when they won the BNFL National Cup, but they lost their grip on that trophy, also on Humberside, going down to Hull NDLB in the quarter-finals. That round proved to be something of a disaster for the National League teams. They could have had four in the semi-finals which would have been just the boost the National League wanted if only to answer those people who believe that there are better teams in other regional leagues than some National sides. But they all went out. Crosfields won at Woolston, and Askam and Kells had home wins over Leigh Miners and West Hull respectively.

There had been a record entry for the 1988–89 National Cup, with 186 clubs, including ten from London. Three of them pulled off superb wins in the first round: Hornsey Lambs beat the well established Redhill (Castleford) 19–0; South London defeated Roose (Barrow) 22–8; and St Mary's College, Twickenham beat Haresfinch (St Helens) 16–8. St Mary's produced an even bigger shock in the second round where only a last-minute disputed try sent them to a 13–16 defeat against the Humberside premier division club, Jesmond.

The National finals day in May turned out to be a super double triumph for North-West Counties teams and misery for Kells. More than 500 fans travelled from Cumbria to see Kells try to do what no other club had done before – win the open age and youth titles on the same day. As it turned out Crosfields won the BNFL National Cup by 25–11 while Widnes Tigers took the National Youth Cup by 19–16 despite the fact that Kells included four players who had been selected for BARLA's tour to Australia.

Tigers became only the second team to win county and national cups in the same season, Wigan St Patrick's being the first. They had much more pace and flair and had the game sewn up by half-time when they led 18–6. The crucial score came right on half-time when Tigers' tourist prop, Peter Ashcroft, showed the pace of a centre to set up a try for Stuart Spruce. Two minutes after the break came the killer with the lively second row, Francis Fenlom, going over.

The man-of-the-match award went to the loose forward, Shaun Donnelly, but there were other candidates including winger Darren O'Brien, Spruce, Atherton and Fenlom. The stand-off, Ian Maher, went off injured after twenty minutes but the way he started he might well have won it. Tigers' tries came from Spruce (2), Michael Riley, O'Brien, Fenlom, Horabin and Atherton, Donnelly kicking five goals and a drop-goal. Wayne Kitchin, Stephen Briscoe and Chris Stables crossed for Kells and Stephen Wear kicked two goals. After the game Darren O'Brien was invited to join the tour squad.

It was a memorable season for Kells who became the first amateur club to have both open-age and youth teams in the National Cup finals. They also provided no fewer than five players for the BARLA Young Lions tour: one was the skilful centre or stand-off, Steve Wear, in action here against Oldham St Anne's in the National Youth Cup semi-final.

In the open-age final, Crosfields were never behind after a second-minute penalty by Mike Redmond but they had to work mighty hard for their win and had to produce all their fine defensive qualities to keep Kells at bay, particularly the Cumbrians' inside backs. Their international centre, Ian Clarke, was always a threat and he got Kells's opening try. But the crucial point came in the forty-ninth minute when the Kells substitute forward, Paul Messenger, who had only been on a few minutes, was sent off and at the same time their skipper and livewire stand-off, Peter Smith, was carried off injured.

Kells battled bravely on and with only five minutes left the Warrington side were still only 13–11 ahead. But then substitute Terry Litz, who had only just got over a serious back injury, stormed forty yards to set up a try for Tony Parker. Two minutes later, he took a short pass from Geoff Clarke to race in. Karl Taylor and Alan Greaves got Crosfields' earlier tries with Redmond kicking four goals and a drop-goal. Chris Kelly was Kells's other try-scorer and Ron Connor kicked a goal. Ian Gainford also dropped a goal. The teams that day in the youth final were:

Widnes Tigers: Lunt; O'Brien, Sharpe, Riley, Stephens; Maher, Spruce; Horabin, Darren Pitt, Atherton, Fenlom, Clare, Donnelly

Substitutes: Stephen Pitt, Mullen

Kells: Burns; Dixon, Huddleston, Rudd, Briscoe; Wear, Kitchin; Seager, Cunningham, Chambers, Neill, Burns, Elliott

Substitutes: Stables, Skelly

In the open-age final the teams were:

Crosfields: Redmond; Vernon, Parker, Greaves, Taylor; Isherwood, Wood; Lomax, Barber, Terry Reid, David Reid, Rourke, Pucill

Substitutes: Clarke, Litz

Kells: Hunter; Connor, Clarke, Seeds, Steward; Smith, Kilpatrick; Doran, Batey, Kenmare, Kelly, Sparks, Gainford

Substitutes: Milburn, Messenger

Referee: C. Smith

Attendance: approx. 5,000

Barrow Island pulled off the biggest shock in the county competitions when they took the Cumbria Cup to Barrow for the first time. They upset all the forecasts and beat Kells, who had won the competition five times before, 18–10 despite having Tammy Tyson sent off in the fourteenth minute. Barrow Island scored three brilliant tries to Kells's one, with Bill Oxley setting up the match winner for Keith Ward in the second half and Dickinson adding his second goal.

Two goals from Weir had put Barrow Island in arrears early on, but then Fell scooped up a loose ball to race over and Dickinson's goal kick put Island ahead. Oxley opened up the way for the second try, scored by the man-of-the-match, their stand-off Graham Dale. Just before half-time, however, Clarke snapped up a loose ball to cross for Kells and Dickinson's goal sent the teams in level at half-time. Any fears that Barrow would run out of steam were ill founded as Ward romped in for the winner.

Thatto Heath, hot favourites for the Burtonwood Lancashire Cup, got a bit of a scare against Leigh East before running out 32–12 winners at Knowsley Road. East had led 12–4 at one point, thanks to tries by Steve Grimshaw and David Kay, both of which Kay goaled. It was the Heath scrum-half, Neil Slater, who turned the game upside down with a try three minutes from half-time which Mark Cook goaled from the touchline. During the first eight minutes of the second half, Slater had gone in for another try and had set one up for Paul Richardson. Eddie Tinsley and Martin Ford added to the try tally – and Cook kicked six goals – as Heath picked up the only trophy they had never won before. But Leigh East didn't deserve to be beaten by 20 points.

The National League side, West Hull, found themselves in a similar position to Thatto Heath in a cracking Bass Yorkshire Cup final. They were 2–11 down to the Yorkshire League senior division side, Hunslet Junction, but steadied themselves to win 32–21 at Elland Road. Junction had gone ahead with tries by Glen Delaney and Vince Nickle, with Neil Wilkinson adding one goal and Nigel Moss dropping a goal. Just when Junction were beginning to look unstoppable, West Hull showed all their expertise to score 18 points in a matter of minutes with tries from Mark Wildridge, man-of-the-match Roy Smallbones, and Carl Newlove, all of which Gary Lumb goaled. Nickle got another try back but that was as close as Hunslet got after having John Linley and John Munnelly sent off.

The victories for Barrow Island, Thatto Heath and West Hull took them into the preliminary round of the Silk Cut Challenge Cup along with last season's National champions, Milford. Thatto Heath almost caused a major upset in the Challenge Cup. After winning 18–11 at Barrow Island in the preliminary round, they went to Chorley in the first round and lost by only 4–8. For long spells in the second half the professionals had to defend desperately to survive. However, West Hull and Milford didn't do so well in their preliminary-round games. West Hull lost 2–48 and missed the chance to face Wigan – while Milford crashed 0–36 at home to Swinton.

St Patrick's and Elland, last season's National Cup finalists, were paired in the first round of the John Player Trophy. It turned out to be a bit of an anti-climax with a much changed Elland side losing 8–36. Knowing that the winners had been drawn away to Sheffield Eagles, both teams had asked the Eagles to give up ground advantage for the first round because they could get bigger gates at their home towns. Needless to say the offer was declined, and Eagles finished up trouncing the Wiganers 86–0.

In the county Under-19 competitions Widnes Tigers scored in injury time to beat Leigh Miners 26–22 in the Rodstock Lancashire Cup final; Kells beat Askam 16–6 in the Cumbria Cup; and East Park Juniors toppled Dewsbury Moor 18–6 in the Garuda Indonesia Yorkshire Cup.

Incidentally, when Widnes and Leigh Miners met again in the Inter-League final, with virtually the same sides as played in the county final, Leigh gained some revenge with a 39–14 win. The Leigh Miners' Great Britain stand-off, Tommy Martyn, scored two tries and five goals to be man-of-the-match.

On the international front most of the emphasis was on the build-up to the 1989 summer youth tour of Australia. The international in France was lost 10–18. Oldham St Anne's scrum-half, Neil Flanagan, who won the man-of-the-match award, got the opening try, goaled by Graham Hallas (Dudley Hill), and Leigh Miners' stand-off, Tommy Martyn, crossed in the second half. Great Britain got their revenge a few weeks later at Featherstone when they beat the French 24–22 with their captain and centre, Alan Hunte, scoring three tries. Kells's centre, Chris Rudd, also got a try and Tommy Martyn kicked three goals. It was a superb win because the French included twelve of their Under-21 side which had defeated the British professionals 16–8 a month earlier.

The original squad for Australia was picked early in the season and was then whittled down to twenty-six players. In fact, with several of the lads having joined professional clubs on amateur forms, the final squad looked pretty strong. Among them was Blackbrook's Gary Connolly, who had not only signed for St Helens but had played full-back against Wigan in the Silk Cut Challenge Cup final. Eastmoor's Alan Hunte had also joined Saints and figured in some end-of-season games including those against Wigan and Widnes. Several other players made senior debuts and BARLA officials hoped that the

One of the country's outstanding players in the National Amateur League was Millom's Peter Knowles, pictured here running strongly in a league match against Dudley Hill. Knowles was capped by BARLA against Papua New Guinea as far back as 1979, as an outstanding goal-kicking full-back. He now operates mainly as a back-row forward.

experience would stand them in good stead to take on the Aussies.

The squad finally chosen to tour was: Peter Atherton (Widnes Tigers), Darren O'Brien (Widnes Tigers), Richard Brook (Dewsbury Moor), Shaun Brown (Leigh East), Steve Burnell (East Leeds), Gary Chambers (Kells), Gary Connelly (Blackbrook), Tony Conroy (Wigan St Patrick's), Jason Critchley (Blackbrook), Paul Darbyshire (Wigan St Patrick's), Martin Eldon (Wath Brow), Dave Elliott (Kells), Stephen Entwistle (Waterhead), Neil Flanagan (Oldham St Anne's), Paul Fletcher (East Park), Alan Hunte (Eastmoor), Martin Kay (Oldham St Anne's), Wayne Kitchen (Wath Brow), Simon Longstaff (Leeds Polytechnic), Karl Marriott (Mayfield), Tommy Martyn (Leigh Miners Welfare), Chris Rudd (Kells), Andrew Southwell (Ellenborough), Stephen Wear (Kells), Barry Williams (Broughton Red Rose).

However, for BARLA's open-age team, it was very much a year to forget. Teams from this side of the Channel are never sure what to expect when they play France – especially when the French are facing a hat-trick of international defeats. Well, on this occasion, Britain crashed to a record 0–62 defeat but to their astonishment found that the French team contained seven internationals who had appeared against the full Great Britain side in the 1989 Tests.

On other fronts, there was an inaugural 'Heart of England' Nines competition at Birmingham with Countesthorpe of Leicester beating Nottingham 12–4 in the final; Bath, almost old hands at Rugby League now, opened their own clubhouse, entertaining the North-West Counties' side, Nutgrove, for the occasion – and later played a return friendly as a curtain-raiser at Knowsley Road. BARLA themselves said goodbye to their old premises in Britannic Buildings, Huddersfield to move a hundred yards down the road to a new £250,000 detached building in order to house properly the growing staff needed to cope with the game's expansion at amateur level.

Another important decision, and the note on which to end this chapter, was BARLA's decision to form a second division in the National League. Two more clubs, Lock Lane and Mayfield, were added to the original ten in the first division. And Askam, Barrow Island, Blackbrook, British Aerospace (Oldham), Crosfields, East Leeds, Leigh East, Redhill (Castleford), Saddleworth, and Shaw Cross were selected to form the second division. However, Crosfields and Blackbrook later pulled out to be replaced by Dewsbury Celtic and Knottingley.

SEVEN

The Student Rugby League World Cup 1989

Mike Rylance

In unfamiliar midsummer, Student Rugby League reached the highest point in its twenty-year history. The biggest event ever staged at this level took place when the Student World Cup competition was held during the early part of August. The tournament also had the distinction of bringing together the largest number of countries to play Rugby League in a single event. Based at York University, representative teams from the four home countries were joined by those from Australia, New Zealand, France and Holland. The only regret was that the Papua-New Guinea students, adrift without funds at the other end of the world, could not raise the finance and the number of participating countries to nine.

But there were other notable firsts, in the shape of the Irish and Dutch teams. The Irish, represented by students in higher education establishments in both Ireland and mainland Britain, were playing as comparative novices but were able to call on the assistance of their compatriot and Britain's national development officer, Tom O'Donovan, and other regional development officers, in order to hasten their progress. Their fellow-initiates, Holland, were practically as green as the Irish, though so enthusiastic to play Rugby League that they chose to take part in preference to their planned Rugby Union tour. They too were grateful for the guidance of their mentor, Tas Baitieri, the former French national team coach and now the International Board's European liaison officer.

What will come of these initiatives no one can say, but like other students new to the game the Irish and Dutch will have returned to their countries having gained pleasure and perhaps enlightenment from their contact with the sport. Far from devaluing the competition by their inexperience, they added interest, colour and variety and, we hope, may add to the future development of Rugby League.

If the Dutch and the Irish made some of the other teams look like old hands, the Scottish team, put together for the first time less than two years ago, were almost as new, with their most experienced player having a career total of just seven matches behind him. Like many other student teams, what they lack in experience they make up for in enthusiasm and commitment. That is also true of the Welsh, who can be relied upon to take their rugby seriously. Coached by Clive Griffiths, formerly of St Helens, now at Warrington, they had the advantage of some key players with genuine Rugby League backgrounds.

The more experienced and longer established teams were always going to be favourites. New Zealand had won the inaugural competition on home soil three years before; Australia, though established fairly recently at this level, can always put out a strong national side in whatever competition they enter. France, who, with England, are one of the oldest Student Rugby League countries, have almost invariably been a good match for anyone, sometimes fielding senior international players, who of course are able to compete at this level because all Rugby League players in France are amateurs. England themselves, under the direction of the ex-Cambridge University coach, Mike Penistone, have gone from strength to strength and the level of play, as reflected in representative matches throughout the year, has improved continually.

This was a bold and ambitious initiative on the part of Bob Ashby and David Oxley in accepting the international board's invitation to stage the tournament and by the RFL's board in agreeing to meet the heavy financial commitment involved. Needless to say, those initiatives were enthusiastically supported by the hard working executive of the Student Rugby League. Generously backed by the highly professional main sponsors, the NatWest Bank, it was a larger undertaking in all respects than the first World Cup competition in New Zealand which had determined the British Students to try to stage the next one.

The organiser employed to manage the event, Bev Risman, was also at the centre of another of the Student Rugby League's ambitions which was realised during the summer. He and Malcolm Reid, the Scottish Students' coach, were nominated as associate directors of the Students' governing body, to be jointly responsible for the development of the sport in universities, colleges and sixth-forms. Both have wide experience of coaching, of the professional game and of working in higher education. A former British Lions captain, Bev Risman has coached recently at Fulham and has been involved in the National Coaching Scheme; he was a lecturer in physical education at West London Institute. Malcolm Reid, who holds a doctorate in psychology, played as a professional with Barrow and was until recently assistant director of physical education at Aberdeen University.

Their appointment represents another stage in the progress of Student Rugby League. The executive body has long recognised the need, and has campaigned, for the appointment of paid officials who can devote themselves fully to the demands of the student game. Working on a voluntary basis, the executive had probably done all it could; though in organising some thirty clubs the length and breadth of Britain it had made truly remarkable strides forward. The time was right for professional support in order to consolidate and develop what had already been achieved.

Sadly there are some who fail to see the significance or relevance of Student Rugby League to the sport as a whole. Today's students, banal as it may be to say so, are tomorrow's decision-makers and so are in a position to influence the progress of the sport, either in its administration, its teaching or its media presentation. At the very least, the newly-appointed associate directors will aim to establish, in Mal Reid's words, 'informed observers', who will play their part in dispelling the ignorance about the game which still exists, near and far.

The Student Rugby League World Cup 1989

The draw for the 1989 Student World Cup was as follows:

Monday 31 July	Scotland v Ireland (Pool B) Heworth Australia v England (Pool B) Heworth
Tuesday 1 August	New Zealand v France (Pool A) Leigh Miners Wales v Holland (Pool A) Bramley
Thursday 3 August	Australia v Scotland (Pool B) Featherstone England v Ireland (Pool B) Warrington
Friday 4 August	New Zealand v Wales (Pool A) Oldham France v Holland (Pool A) Wakefield
Sunday 6 August	Australia v Ireland (Pool B) St Helens England v Scotland (Pool B) St Helens
Monday 7 August	New Zealand v Holland (Pool A) Halifax France v Wales (Pool A) Widnes
Wednesday 9 August	*Semi-Finals*: Winner (Pool A) v Runner-up (Pool B) Doncaster *Semi-Finals*: Winner (Pool B) v Runner-up (Pool A) Swinton
Friday 11 August	3rd in Pool A v 3rd in Pool B Heworth 4th in Pool A v 4th in Pool B Heworth
Saturday 12 August	3rd/4th place play-off: Central Park, Wigan Grand Final: Central Park, Wigan

The tournament was not only a success beyond expectation, it was also a unique Rugby League experience. Played by intelligent, articulate young men who showed real sportsmanship and dedication, the matches delighted an appreciative public and gained extensive and sympathetic media coverage. The fact that Australia emerged as champions after a closely contested final with England was almost irrelevant. What was important was the spirit evident throughout the competition and, perhaps especially, the commitment of the new countries and the high level of skill they achieved after such a short time. It was a competition in which all who were involved felt proud to take part and which will win many friends for Rugby League.

In the Grand Final Australia beat England 10–5; and in the 3rd/4th play-off match France beat New Zealand 28–16.

EIGHT

The New Frontiers

Huw Richards

Earlier in the year the theatregoers' group in the Shropshire market town of Bridgnorth planned one of their regular Friday night outings. The chosen play featured the 'Allo, 'Allo star, Gordon Kaye, and there were eighty-one bookings – about average for the group. But plans fell through, leaving the organisers to look for alternatives in the West Midlands. They settled on Hull Truck's touring production of John Godber's Rugby League epic *Up and Under*. The eighty-one takers were offered a choice – either their money back or *Up and Under*. Only thirty-four opted for *Up and Under*.

The people who rejected John Godber's play were not expressing anti-League sentiments or solidarity with the town's Union club. They were just not interested: League had no part in their lives. In nearly 100 years the game has made no impact on their town, yet Bridgnorth is less than 100 miles from notable League centres like Warrington and Widnes.

While 'Victorian values' has been one of the catchphrases of the 1980s, for Rugby League it is more a case of 'Victorian boundaries'. To a remarkable extent the code's development is defined by the great schism of 1895, powerful in the environs of clubs which went with the broken-time payers of the Northern Union and of little or no significance elsewhere. There have been odd advances and retreats from the precise lines of 1895. But plot them on a map and it is easy to believe that League – like the Gaelic sports and, until recently, American Football – has been content to stay self-sufficient within historic boundaries, making little or no attempt to encroach on the rest of the world.

Of course that could hardly be further from the truth. Ever since it became clear that there would be no reconciliation between the rival versions of rugby, League has battled to expand beyond its heartland. For the first ninety years of League history two policies were tried. The first was the 'missionary' game, taking an outstanding game to new areas in the hope that the sight of top performers would inspire watchers to play the game themselves. The second method was to encourage professional sides outside the heartlands. Two target areas in particular have always appealed – Wales with its massive stocks of rugby talent and social similarities with the northern heartlands, and London, partly for its huge population but more for its domination of the nation's media and commerce.

Only once has professional Rugby League truly succeeded in extending its British boundaries, moving up the Cumbrian coast after the Second World War to admit first Workington and then Whitehaven. But there had been a Millom club in the early years – and the two newcomers could call on some powerful local amateur talent. The 1930s tactic of planting professional franchises in virgin territory lived on intermittently into the 1980s. Starting with Fulham in 1980, a series of clubs entered the league, piggybacked on the existing name and facilities of soccer clubs. Fulham and Carlisle enjoyed early successes but partnerships were short-lived and unhappy as soccer clubs inevitably and naturally put their own game first. Only at Elland Road, where Hunslet have a long-established local identity, and council ownership avoids landlord-tenant tensions between the two games, has a League-soccer share worked for any length of time.

After ninety years of unavailing attempts to force the growth of League through professional clubs, unsupported by existing local interest or any amateur infrastructure, the lesson has been learned. Gary Hetherington, whose Sheffield Eagles are the happy exception to most rules about the new clubs of the 1980s, now says: 'If I started again, I'd build a decent amateur base before I ever attempted to set up a professional club.'

That view has belatedly become the conventional wisdom. The odds have always been against the professional game generating serious development in virgin territory. The horizons of professional clubs are inevitably short-term and self-centred, driven by external commercial imperatives. Exclusively northern, based on and controlled by a network of professional clubs, the Rugby Football League was never likely to regard development as a major priority. Detached observers in Australia have criticised the League for failure to give the Fulham club more support, but the Chapeltown Road hierachy have been aware that any special assistance can be regarded by their members as giving an unfair advantage to a competitor. Far from helping the game expand, it can be argued that the League failed before 1973 even to safeguard the amateur game in the heartlands.

Amateur Rugby League, free from commercial constraints, has always offered a more promising long-term route to territorial expansion. Now a commitment to national development, implicit in BARLA's brief since its foundation in 1973, has taken shape in the last few years through national coaching and development schemes. That commitment led, early in 1988, to the appointment of Tom O'Donovan as the first BARLA National Development Officer, charged with the formidable task of making League a national game in time for its centenary in 1995. That target does not imply expectations that the professional league should have a national network to match soccer's within seven years – clearly an impossibility – but the more modest target of establishing a credible presence in every major centre of population.

A year on, and with 28,000 miles on the clock of his car in rather less than twelve months, O'Donovan could say: 'It has become clear quite how formidable the task is.' That year has seen him on the road, travelling to the game's furthest-flung outposts, meeting the people who keep the game going and assessing their needs. The boost for morale in those areas, with the realisation that somebody in the north does care what they are doing, has been considerable. But the weight of expectation placed on Tom O'Donovan should not be underestimated.

Priorities for the coming year will include a drive to make people in the traditional League areas more aware of the game's existence in other regions. 'Many people simply don't know that Rugby League exists in London, East

Anglia, the Midlands or the West Country. They may be lost to the game if they move to those areas, or even deterred from moving by the belief that there is no League,' says Tom. This drive will be backed by an information system that can rapidly tell callers to BARLA headquarters in Huddersfield where clubs and enthusiasts in the development regions can be found.

London remains the key target, a priority reaffirmed just before last Christmas by the appointment of Ken Johnson, a thirty-two-year-old teacher, as the London Development Officer – the first to be employed directly by BARLA rather than by a local authority. Like Tom O'Donovan, an Irishman from Limerick, Ken Johnson, as a native of Durham, brings to his post the perceptions of someone who grew up in an area without RL traditions.

Amateur RL maintains a tenacious toehold on the capital and its environs, with sixteen teams competing in the 1988–89 London Amateur Rugby League. That season saw a particularly encouraging spread into Essex and East Anglia, with Essex Scimitars and Cambridge City Tigers showing considerable promise in their début seasons. Less happily, Ipswich, playing friendlies under the direction of the controversial former Kent Invicta and Fulham owner, Paul Faires, ended the season under suspension by the LARL.

Australians and New Zealanders maintain a prominent role in the Stones Bitter London League. The League champions, Hemel Hempstead, returning to London after a spell in the Midlands and South-West ARL, included a number of Australians and New Zealanders. London Colonials, predominantly Australian, and South London Wanderers, made up mainly of New Zealanders, have been the dominant force of recent years. In 1988–89 they recovered after slow starts and came through to contest a fierce Unity Bank Cup final, played for the second year running in true ecumenical spirit on the ground of Wasps FC, South London winning 26–22. That trio has now been challenged by St Mary's College and Fulham Travellers, completing the most powerful top five in the League's history.

Dramatic evidence of improving standards came in the BARLA National Cup. Until recently London's ambitions had been limited to the hope that their very best teams might ambush someone from the lower divisions of the northern leagues. But this season saw St Mary's, South London and, most spectacular of all, Hornsey Lambs beating strong northern opponents. Lambs – their name a satire on rugby macho – put aside disappointing LARL form in a staggering 19–0 victory over Redhill of Castleford, subsequently selected for a BARLA National League place.

London clubs also showed a commitment to development elsewhere, with Hemel Hempstead and Hornsey crossing the North Sea at Easter for a first-ever Dutch RL tournament that took place near Amsterdam. Hemel emerged as winners after a hugely succesful and entertaining couple of days, in which the Dutch sides, plus a number of German enthusiasts distributed among the competing teams, showed much promise.

There are numerous problems to preoccupy Ken Johnson. Too many London clubs are one or two-man operations – over-dependent on a key enthusiast. South London, for example, the capital's most succesful club since the mid-1980s, came close to collapse following the departure in 1988 of their secretary, Mel Wibberley. Moreover, most clubs are open-age only, offering

South London Wanderers break clear to score on their way to a close win over their rivals London Colonials in the Unity Trust Bank London Challenge Cup final.

little opportunity to young players not yet ready for the challenge of adult RL.

Only Hemel Hempstead, with two open-age sides, a range of youth teams and a clubhouse, come close to matching conditions that will be demanded of applicants for the BARLA National League if their ambition of linking a southern premier division to the national structure is achieved.

Schools RL in the south is extremely limited, with the setting up of the St Mary's, Hendon team, among the competitors at Ken Johnson's recent open evening, the one bright spot. Ken sees schools and student teachers as the key to the future: 'Widnes, with about six secondary schools and sixteen amateur clubs, has built great sides on local talent. London has about 250 schools. If we could get twenty playing the game well, a lot of talent would come through,' he says. Supporting evidence shows that a tiny, short-lived London Schools League produced Fulham's first-teamer Andrew Mighty and their reserve Roy Leslie. Persuading London, in its massive indifference, to take notice of League, will be a hard job. Not the least of Ken Johnson's needs will be time and patience on the part of other enthusiasts: the time to judge his efforts will be the end of the century, not the end of next season.

Next in line for a Development Officer is likely to be the Midlands and South-West region – with the Birmingham area the most likely location if and when the Sports Council provides the necessary funding. The Midlands and

South-West Amateur Rugby League Association (MASWARLA) continues to grapple with the logistics of running the game for a vast region extending from Countesthorpe and Wolverhampton in the Midlands to Plymouth in the West and Aberavon in Wales.

Two members of the BARLA Young Lions squad took part in a titanic National Youth Cup semi-final between Kells and Oldham St Anne's. Scrum-half Neil Flanagan (St Anne's) prepares to launch an attack before Kells's loose forward, David Elliott (*left*), can pounce.

It is little wonder that MASWARLA were considering splitting into West and Midlands sections of about six teams each in place of the two-divisional set-up employed in 1988–89. But regional groupings risk mixing too wide a range of abilities, discouraging new teams and failing to stretch the better established. The road to development is paved with such tough marginal decisions.

Bath and Aberavon dominated the MASWARLA League, with Cheltenham Endsleigh, arguably the League's most improved team, their main challenger. Aberavon took the League title and Cup, beating Bath in the final at Stroud, while Bath took the premiership, awarded in the second half of the season. The Aberavon secretary, Danny Sheehy, points to the continuing cost and administrative effort of travelling to England for all their matches. The need for opponents closer to home is desperate, and Danny reckons there is enough playing interest to set up a League club in every Welsh town with a senior Union club – but a complete dearth of prospective administrators and coaches rules this out.

Nor is getting the game into schools a serious possibility in Wales and numerous other Union strongholds in the MASWARLA area. But RL expansion at open-age level continues. Birmingham, the most conspicuous blank on the League map, should be running a team for the first time next year, started by the MASWARLA secretary, John Simkin, after a League open-day at a sports centre in the city. Two other teams should fill in gaps between MAS-WARLA and London, with Southampton joining London and Swindon creating a further link down the M4 towards the capital: 'Reading should be next, and then you're not too far from London's western outpost at Ealing,' says Dave Kay, MASWARLA's honorary Development Officer.

The game in the Midlands suffered a grievous blow with the early death of Dave Pickett, the driving force behind Redditch Halcyon and a former League chairman. But better news was the reformation of the Biddulph club as Stoke Michelin, keeping open-age RL alive in Staffordshire and opting, like Countesthorpe of Leicester, for the Midlands competition rather than the Mansfield League (MANARLA) because of a preference for Sunday games.

MANARLA saw their professional flagship, Mansfield Marksman (now Nottingham City), suffer a more than usually traumatic season, but enjoyed what their secretary-chairman, David Stephenson, reckoned was their best ever year. Clowne Angels won the League, and can look forward to a talented crop of teenage players from the local comprehensive school on the point of breaking through at open-age level. But they were pressed all the way by a vastly improved Nottingham Crusaders. Administrators, coaches and referees – League development's holy trinity of scarce resources – remained, as ever, in short supply.

In Carlisle, by contrast, a league that once boasted ten teams has declined to the extent that it voted to dissolve at the end of the season with the surviving clubs – Dalston A, Legends and St Nicholas Arms – moving into neighbouring Cumbrian competitions. Players who had been the backbone of amateur rugby, since the formation of the city's professional club stimulated expansion after 1981, have been retiring, with no replacements coming through. But all is not lost. Growing activity at junior and schools level promises a resurgence in the near future; Carlisle's problem is a generation gap rather than overall decline.

The same applies in the north-east where Durham, who withdrew from the Carlisle competition, plan three age-group teams in the coming season in spite of leaving open-age competition. Their departure follows the loss, eighteen months ago, of Frankland Prison, following a tightening in prison regulations. Steve Rich, secretary of the Durham club, speaks of 'a few isolated pockets of resistance' in the region with Newcastle, Sunderland and Hartlepool playing in the York and District League. Hartlepool have taken free gangway ecumenism to the extent of happily sharing facilities with a local Union club. Durham's concentration on developing young players is being replicated elsewhere with members of Sunderland and Newcastle looking to introduce the game into local schools.

Steve Rich feels the north-east is sometimes forgotten by BARLA officials looking south for development: 'I feel we've got as far as we can without the stimulus that would be provided by a full-time Development Officer and a professional club in the area,' he says. The model he is looking at is provided further south at Sheffield, where the Eagles and the area Development Officer, Tim Butcher, are making great strides in what was previously a League desert.

Twenty-five primary schools and eleven secondary schools in the city are now playing the game, virtually all of them having started since Tim Butcher's appointment in the last two years. The open-age scene is still limited in Sheffield, but there can be little doubt that many young players will leave school wanting to continue playing, creating the impetus for further development. Rich points to the importance of co-operation between the junior, amateur and professional levels of the game – as exemplified in Sheffield. And looking at likely sites for a future north-eastern professional club, he nominates Darlington.

Quite when and if amateur development leads on to new professional clubs is a question yet to be answered. Steve Rich points out: 'The process by which you set up a professional club seems to be shrouded in a certain amount of mystery.' But at a certain stage it appears to be an essential element in maintaining expansion: 'It makes an enormous difference to youngsters if you can point to a professional level to which they can aspire,' he says.

The 'development' model of RL expansion will certainly take years to produce its first professional club in the outlying areas. But long-term development, based on a firm junior and amateur base, has to be a better bet for the future of the game than the now discredited 'franchise' model.

Much may depend on League's fastest growing sector, the student game. Current employment patterns make it inevitable that the bulk of today's graduates will find jobs in areas outside traditional League heartlands. The key for development is to ensure that student players are kept involved in the game when they leave college, sending shoals of enthusiasts into non-traditional League areas. Our universities, polytechnics and colleges no longer produce thousands of missionaries to take the church's message to Africa and Asia. But there is no reason why today's students should not be missionaries taking League to London, Birmingham, Swansea and Exeter.

The John Player Special Trophy

Preliminary Round	1st round		2nd round		3rd round		Semi-finals		Final	
	York	6	St Helens	16						
	St Helens	14			St Helens	34				
	Hull	26	Hull	13						
	Batley	10					St Helens	18		
	Wakefield T	34	Wakefield T	38						
	Carlisle	14			Wakefield T	18				
	Rochdale H	26	Rochdale H	12					Widnes 6	
	Whitehaven	20								
	Sheffield E	80	Sheffield E	9						
Wigan St Patrick's 36	Wigan St Patrick's	8			Widnes	16				
Elland 2	Widnes	37	Widnes	32						
Featherstone R 46	Featherstone R	12					Widnes	20		
Hunslet 2	Warrington	21	Warrington	42						
	Oldham	14			Warrington	7				
Bramley 56	Bramley	32	Bramley	10						
Fulham 10	Mansfield M	6								
	Leeds	12	Castleford	18						
Workington T 2	Castleford	21			Bradford N	6				
Castleford 28	Bradford N	34	Bradford N	19						
	Dewsbury	18					Bradford N	5		
	Leigh	42	Leigh	40						
	Barrow	14			Leigh	0				
	Swinton	13	Doncaster	8					Wigan 12	
	Doncaster	16								
	Huddersfield	4	Chorley B	22						
	Chorley B	22			Hull KR	16				
	Hull KR	40	Hull KR	36						
	Keighley	0					Wigan	16		
	Runcorn H	2	Wigan	20						
	Wigan	92			Wigan	16				
	Halifax	22	Halifax	16	(Replay: 30–0 to Wigan)					
	Salford	4								

The John Smith's Yorkshire Cup

Preliminary Round	1st round		2nd round		Semi-finals		Final	
	Halifax	36	Halifax	24				
	Batley	14			Halifax	8		
	Keighley	22	Hull KR	2				
	Hull KR	28					Castleford	12
	Castleford	94	Castleford	40				
	Huddersfield	12			Castleford	12		
	York	25	York	14				
	Mansfield M	4						
Bramley 16	Leeds	24	Leeds	15				
Leeds 38	Bradford N	21			Leeds	12		
Sheffield E 8	Wakefield T	46	Wakefield T	10				
Wakefield T 28	Dewsbury	20					Leeds	33
	Hull	53	Hull	18				
	Hunslet	0			Hull	8		
	Featherstone R	38	Featherstone R	0				
	Doncaster	8						

The Grünhalle Lager Lancashire Cup

1st round		2nd round		Semi-finals		Final	
Oldham	64	Oldham	2				
Workington T	2			Salford	15		
Salford	42	Salford	18				
Whitehaven	8					Salford	17
Runcorn H	4	Warrington	34				
Warrington	42			Warrington	2		
Carlisle	17	Carlisle	18				
Chorley B	7						
Barrow	10	Wigan	36				
Wigan	24			Wigan	14		
Rochdale H	25	Rochdale H	4				
Fulham	14					Wigan	22
Widnes	32	Widnes	38				
St Helens	24			Widnes	10		
Swinton	24	Swinton	4				
Leigh	14						

The Silk Cut Challenge Cup

Preliminary Round		1st round		2nd round		3rd round		Semi-finals		Final	
Milford	0	Swinton	5	St Helens	28						
Swinton	36	St Helens	16			St Helens	32				
		Barrow	38	Barrow	6						
		Huddersfield	16					St Helens	16		
Wakefield T	18	Wakefield T	34	Wakefield T	4						
Bramley	10	Batley	4			Featherstone R	3				
		Whitehaven	0	Featherstone R	10						
		Featherstone R	32							St Helens	0
York	35	York	9	Leeds	24						
Workington T	8	Leeds	28			Leeds	4				
Leeds	32	Carlisle	58	Carlisle	4						
Hunslet	6	Mansfield M	1					Widnes	14		
		Hull	4	Castleford	18						
		Castleford	7			Widnes	24				
		Salford	14	Widnes	32						
		Widnes	18								
		Rochdale H	24	Hull KR	28						
		Hull KR	28			Hull KR	4				
		Chorley B	8	Chorley B	4						
Barrow Island	11	Thatto Heath	4					Warrington	6		
Thatto Heath	18	Warrington	25	Warrington	56						
		Halifax	8			Warrington	30				
		Runcorn H	10	Keighley	7						
		Keighley	28							Wigan	27
		Sheffield E	23	Sheffield E	20						
		Leigh	17			Oldham	4				
		Dewsbury	9	Oldham	32						
		Oldham	40					Wigan	13		
		Fulham	10	Bradford N	4						
West Hull	2	Bradford N	28			Wigan	12				
Doncaster	48	Doncaster	6	Wigan	17						
		Wigan	38								

The Stones Bitter Championship
Final League Tables

		P	W	D	L	Points F	A	Pts
Division 1	Widnes	26	20	1	5	726	345	41
	Wigan	26	19	–	7	543	434	38
	Leeds	26	18	–	8	530	380	36
	Hull	26	17	–	9	427	355	34
	Castleford	26	15	2	9	601	480	32
	Featherstone Rovers	26	13	1	12	482	545	27
	St Helens	26	12	1	13	513	529	25
	Bradford Northern	26	11	1	14	545	518	23
	Wakefield Trinity	26	11	1	14	413	540	23
	Salford	26	11	–	15	469	526	22
	Warrington	26	10	–	16	456	455	20
	Oldham	26	8	1	17	462	632	17
	Halifax	26	6	1	19	335	535	13
	Hull Kingston Rovers	26	6	1	19	408	636	13

		P	W	D	L	Points F	A	Pts
Division 2	Leigh	28	26	–	2	925	338	52
	Barrow	28	21	1	6	726	324	43
	Sheffield Eagles	28	19	1	8	669	362	39
	York	28	17	1	10	585	383	35
	Swinton	28	16	2	10	621	482	34
	Doncaster	28	17	–	11	599	464	34
	Whitehaven	28	15	2	11	522	378	32
	Keighley	28	16	–	12	549	525	32
	Rochdale Hornets	28	15	–	13	655	677	30
	Bramley	28	14	1	13	600	514	29
	Carlisle	28	14	1	13	512	441	29
	Batley	28	13	3	12	461	416	29
	Dewsbury	28	13	–	15	518	626	26
	Hunslet	28	12	1	15	472	540	25
	Fulham	28	10	–	18	464	650	20
	Chorley Borough	28	9	1	18	408	533	19
	Workington Town	28	9	1	18	365	549	19
	Huddersfield	28	9	1	18	400	615	19
	Mansfield Marksman	28	4	1	23	308	768	9
	Runcorn Highfield	28	2	1	25	224	998	5

The Stones Bitter Premiership

1st round		Semi-finals		Final	
Hull	32	Hull	23	Hull	10
Castleford	6				
Leeds	12	Featherstone Rovers	0		
Featherstone Rovers	15				
Widnes	30	Widnes	38	Widnes	18
Bradford Northern	18				
Wigan	2	St Helens	14		
St Helens	4				

Second Division

1st round		Semi-finals		Final	
Barrow	30	Barrow	6	Sheffield Eagles	43
Whitehaven	5				
Sheffield Eagles	28	Sheffield Eagles	9		
Doncaster	10				
Leigh	38	Leigh	8	Swinton	18
Keighley	12				
York	4	Swinton	20		
Swinton	4				

(*Replay:* 17–16 to Swinton)

Leading Scorers

Tries

Offiah (Widnes)	60
Ledger (Leigh)	34
Bate (Swinton)	32
Hanley (Wigan)	29
Lister (Bramley)	28
Powell (Sheffield Eagles)	28
Lewis (Bramley)	26
Quirk (St Helens)	24
Anderson (Castleford)	24
Burns (Barrow)	24

Goals

Aston (Sheffield Eagles)	148
Ketteridge (Castleford)	129
Hobbs (Bradford Northern)	118
Johnson (Leigh)	117
Marwood (Barrow)	115
Loughlin (St Helens)	113
Noble (Doncaster)	110
Woods (Warrington)	107
Currier (Widnes)	107
Turner (Rochdale Hornets)	104

Points

	Trs	Gls	Dr.-gls	Pts
Aston (Sheffield Eagles)	6	135	13	307
Currier (Widnes)	19	106	1	289
Johnson (Leigh)	12	114	3	279
Hobbs (Bradford Northern)	10	113	5	271
Ketteridge (Castleford)	3	129	–	270

Martin Offiah was again one of the stars of the
championship season, scoring no less than sixty tries
including a hat-trick for Widnes in the championship
decider against Wigan.

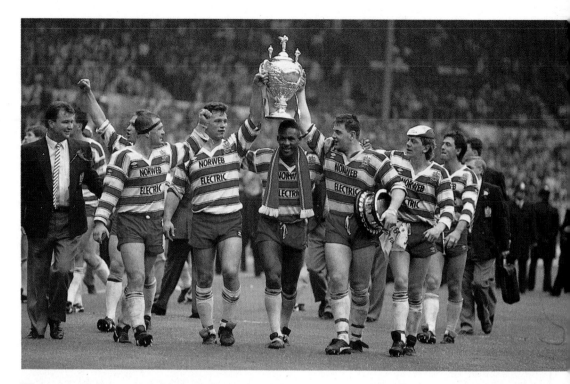

Wigan surpassed themselves in the Challenge Cup final,
playing brilliant rugby to beat St Helens 27–0.
Here they celebrate with a lap of honour,
watched over by their outstanding coach Graham Lowe.

below Shaun Edwards finds a way through
a circle of St Helens defenders in the
Challenge Cup final at Wembley.

Lydon is tackled but keeps possession
Wigan during the Lancashire Cup Final
against Salford, won by Wigan 22–17,

below Ron Gibbs, Castleford's rugged Australian
second-row, evades Cliff Lyons of Leeds
and gets the ball away in the Yorkshire
Cup final, won by Leeds 33–12.

Tony Myler passes on in the Premiership Trophy final against Hull, despite the attentions of Hull's second-row Paul Welham. Widnes won 18–10.

Richard Eyres, supported by scrum-half David Hulme, hands off Hull's Gary Pearce and evades the attentions of their loose forward Gary Divorty in the Premiership Trophy final.

Though tackled, Hugh Waddell keeps his feet and, having pierced the Wigan defence, looks to continue the movement in a Leeds v Wigan championship match.

Paul McDermott with Sonny Nickle (almost off camera) in support, and backed up by three other members of the Sheffield side, appear to have the field to themselves during Sheffield Eagles' great win 43–18 over Swinton in the second-division Premiership final.

Martin Bella, the Queensland prop, charges at the NSW defenders in the third State of Origin match. Bella was selected for the Australian squad to tour New Zealand in July.

Brad Clyde, the Canberra and NSW loose forward, escapes the clutches of Queensland's Paul Vautin during the third State of Origin match. Clyde was Australia's forward discovery of the season, playing outstandingly well in both the State of Origin and NZ Test series.

Ellery Hanley, Great Britain's captain, lifts the trophy after Great Britain had defeated the Rest of the World 30–28 at Headingley.

The NSW captain, Gavin Miller, goes past Dan Stains, the Queensland forward, in the third State of Origin match.

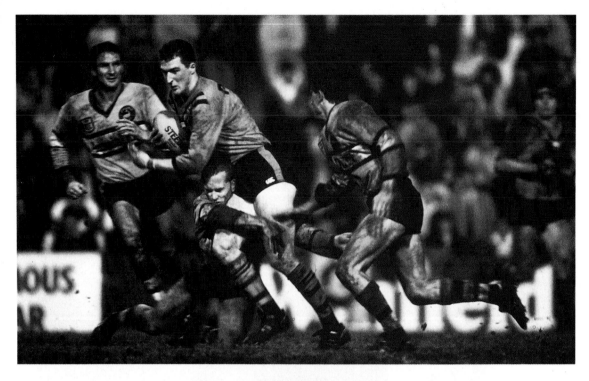

Andy Currier, of Widnes, races way for Balmain in a league match against Cronulla during his summer stint in Australia.

Ellery Hanley was the first British player to win the prestigious Golden Boot award, as the world's most outstanding player during 1988–89. The presentation was made in Australia when Hanley was playing for Wests.

2

The International Scene

ONE

Great Britain's Internationals 1988–89

Harry Edgar

For the next twelve months, the men in black from New Zealand will play an important part in the life and times of Great Britain's Rugby League team. First, the Kiwis come to Europe then, at the end of the 1989–90 season, the Lions undertake their first major tour of New Zealand.

Few individuals are better qualified to assess the current merits of British and New Zealand Rugby League than Graham Lowe. His highly successful three years as Wigan coach were preceded by a similar period as the charismatic figurehead of Kiwi Rugby League.

Lowe, like most wise judges, anticipates a closely fought Test series in October and November. In the three years since he left New Zealand to join Wigan he has seen the game in Britain progress remarkably. 'I think that's because the majority of teams are far better organised than they used to be,' says Lowe. 'When I first came to Britain there was nothing wrong with the standard of fitness or skills of the players here; the major improvements have been in the preparation of teams and in the planning of the game.

'Now I'm sure the top English clubs could compete with, and beat, the Sydney clubs. Anyone can see how the game is coming along in leaps and bounds in Britain. But, unfortunately for the British, the respective standards of the game in different nations is always going to be judged on Test performances – and, in recent years, that's where Britain has fallen down badly against the Australians.'

Few observers would disagree with Graham Lowe's opinion that 'now British Rugby League has every reason to be confident of changing those Test results. There have been obvious improvements in the game here, and there's an impressive breed of excellent young players coming through. Britain has immense potential; it's all down to getting their team selection right and picking the form players for Test matches.'

Just as any nation's standards will be measured by their success or failure in Test matches, it is equally certain that the quality of any international side is a direct result of the overall strength of the domestic competition its players are involved in on a weekly basis. Frank Stanton always emphasised that point when his 1982 'Invincibles' were sweeping all before them in this country with a brand of football that sent shock waves reverberating throughout European Rugby League.

While Great Britain and New Zealand will always find themselves united in one common aim – that of 'beating the Aussies' – both now have strong cause to thank the Australians for provoking and influencing the positive changes recently implemented in the other League-playing countries.

As Graham Lowe says, the British club competition is now of such an intensely high standard that success in an Ashes series should be seen as a confidently attainable target rather than just the forlorn dream it was for Great Britain teams throughout most of the 1980s. Likewise, New Zealand's Test team started to become a formidable force as more and more of their players went overseas to play as professionals in either Britain or Australia.

Discussion of the international season is always going to be put in the context of Great Britain catching up after the nightmare years that followed the 1978 and 1982 Kangaroo tours. It took quite a while for the message to get through, and New Zealand seemed to be a good deal more capable of putting their house in order than Great Britain for a few painful years. But now, the international arena is bubbling with excitement, in the knowledge that a highly competitive Test series will draw huge crowds.

The progress made by British Rugby League can be mirrored by the change in close-season activity of the leading players. Since the watershed of 1982, British Test hopefuls have spent each summer in training camps, desperately trying to bring their standards of conditioning up to the levels demanded by international Rugby League in the modern era.

This year, however, Phil Larder, the national director of coaching and assistant Test coach, was proud to announce that there was no need for special summer training squads for would-be international players, because all the top clubs were now aware of the requirements and were implementing the kind of schedules needed. Added to this, of course, many of Britain's Test players are now playing successfully for leading Australian clubs – something that would have been hard to imagine just four or five years ago.

Moreover, in June, Ellery Hanley became the first British player to win the Adidas Golden Boot award as the world's best player. This coveted award, the symbol of worldwide excellence in Rugby League, was created by *Open Rugby* magazine, and is presented by them in association with Adidas, and *Rugby League Week* and Channel Ten in Australia. Hanley was overjoyed at being named officially as the world's best, ahead of such illustrious rivals as Wally Lewis, Gavin Miller, Ben Elias and Allan Langer. Few could argue with the choice of the Great Britain captain after his memorable efforts in 1988–89, which included taking the Lance Todd Trophy for Wigan at Wembley, inspiring Balmain to the Sydney Grand Final and skippering Britain to their first Test win over Australia for a decade. He was the sixth winner, following in the footsteps of Wally Lewis, Brett Kenny, Garry Jack, Hugh McGahan and Peter Sterling.

British Rugby League clubs made their first appearance on American soil when Wigan beat Warrington 12–5 before 17,773 wildly enthusiastic spectators in Milwaukee's County Stadium on 10 June. The crowd gave the teams a five-minute standing ovation after watching a full-blooded encounter between these two fierce rivals on a balmy summer evening.

Only one try was scored in a game that had been billed as the great American Challenge match. Andy Goodway recorded the historic touchdown while all Wigan's other points came from the boot of Joe Lydon. For Warrington, John Woods kicked two penalties and their scrum-half, Robert Turner, landed a drop-goal. Mike Gregory was voted man-of-the-match by British and Ameri-

Tony Iro, Wigan's New Zealand winger, faces a tackle head on during the American Challenge match at Milwaukee.

John Woods, who played consistently well for Warrington throughout the season, looks to pass and to avoid a tackle from Wigan's Dennis Betts, in the American Challenge match.

can media personnel.

The game was the first to be staged by the United States Rugby League, a largely British-owned company driven on by the tireless determination of its founder and president Michael Mayer. After twelve years of trying to raise funding and British enthusiasm to stage a major game on American soil, Mayer finally achieved his initial goal, thanks to the commitment of the Wigan and Warrington clubs.

After the reaction of the crowd and media to the Milwaukee match all Mayer's predictions about the potential for Rugby League in the U.S. were proved correct. The game now has a great opportunity to develop if it can follow up this first initiative with another game next year, promoted on a much bigger scale and staged almost certainly in Chicago.

Mark Preston, Wigan, charges away from Des Drummond and John Woods during the Milwaukee match.

It would have been dangerous for the British to place too much store on the memory of their third Test win in Sydney last year if firm evidence of progress on other fronts had not followed in the next twelve months. Generally, results on that 1988 Lions tour were pretty disastrous, with credibility only rescued by that emotional victory in a largely empty Sydney Football Stadium in the last game in Australia. Britain's morale-boosting Test win was put into better perspective three months later when a much more wisely selected Australian side hammered New Zealand in the World Cup final in Auckland.

Before they arrive in Europe early in the new season, the Kiwis will have played a three-match home series against the Australians. If they emerge well from that series, Great Britain's motivation to beat them will be that much stronger.

In international Rugby League, one eye is always going to be turned towards the Australians and the next time one has to play them. They are the yardstick by which every other nation must measure its standards. So Britain's meeting with the Kiwis in 1989 and 1990 will still be seen as an aperitif to the main event – the 1990 Ashes series against the Kangaroos.

With British Rugby League now in such confident mood, they will host the New Zealanders in the strong belief that they can win a home Test series for the first time since 1965. While it is common knowledge that Britain have not won the Ashes at home since 1959, not so widely mentioned is their failure to beat the last three Kiwi touring teams – New Zealand won in 1971, and both the 1980 and 1985 series were drawn.

The platform of two confident wins over France earlier in the year helped Malcolm Reilly and his Great Britain team to re-group after the Lions tour. The record 30–8 triumph in Avignon, in particular, showed Britain in a mature, well organised mood rarely seen before on French soil from British teams. Now, much more substantial challenges lie ahead.

GREAT BRITAIN v THE REST OF THE WORLD

Headingley,
Leeds,
29 October

Great Britain 30 Rest of the World XIII 28

In the aftermath of the 1988 Lions tour, and with no major in-coming tour to Europe that autumn, Great Britain's 1988–89 international season was destined to be low key – perhaps a time for reflection after the long haul through Australasia.

Certainly, nostalgia and reflection were the order of the day at the opening of Rugby League's Hall of Fame, a shrine to the great men and deeds in the history of the game. As a focal point of the opening celebrations, a Rest of the World team was assembled to play Great Britain at Headingley.

Rugby League fans are spoilt by the free running entertainment their sport provides, even in the tensest, most hard fought encounters. Unlike Rugby Union followers, who use 'Barbarian'-type fixtures to enjoy attacking play rarely seen in seriously competitive matches, League people are reluctant to support anything they sense to be an 'exhibition' game. That was what happened with this Great Britain versus Rest of the World encounter. Despite considerable publicity and the controversial postponement of the entire first division championship programme for that weekend, just over 12,000 spectators turned out at Headingley. Many more, of course, chose to stay at home and watch the game on live television.

The Rest of the World selection was shorn of much of its public attraction when a broken arm, sustained in the World Cup final, ruled out Wally Lewis.

Gavin Miller, for so long a stalwart of the Australian and Hull KR sides, played for the Rest of the World against Great Britain in the Hall of Fame celebration game at Headingley. Here he looks to pass before being tackled by Leeds's Roy Powell. Miller continues to show his skills for Cronulla in the Sydney League.

Instead it was the Kiwi, Mark Graham, at the time playing for Wakefield Trinity, who captained a Rest of the World team low on practice, and in some cases match fitness, but high on natural talent.

Great Britain took the game very seriously, and while showing some excellent attacking play, must have left their coach, Malcolm Reilly, a little perturbed at the defensive work which allowed the hastily gathered Rest of the World outfit to break through for five tries of their own. In the event, only a missed touchline conversion attempt by Michael O'Connor in the dying moments prevented a draw at 30 points each. That result would have stretched credibility just a bit too far, in a game that was highly entertaining, seriously fought, but obviously lacking in passion.

Another mighty front-rower's performance from Kevin Ward, and the return to the international side of Shaun Edwards, were Great Britain's major points of note in a 30–28 victory.

Great Britain: Loughlin (St Helens); Plange (Castleford), Schofield (Leeds), Stephenson (Leeds), Offiah (Widnes); Edwards (Wigan), Andy Gregory (Wigan); Ward (Castleford), Kevin Beardmore (Castleford), Waddell (Leeds), Mike Gregory (Warrington), Platt (Wigan), Hanley (Wigan)

Substitutes: David Hulme (Widnes), Powell (Leeds)

Scorers: tries – Schofield, Offiah, Hanley, Stephenson, Edwards; goals – Stephenson (5)

Rest of the World: Shearer (Australia); Krewanty (Papua New Guinea), Numapo (Papua New Guinea), O'Connor (Australia), Ratier (France); Ella (Australia), Langer (Australia); Kurt Sorensen (New Zealand), Valero (France), Backo (Australia), Graham (New Zealand), Cleal (Australia), Miller (Australia)

Substitutes: Brown (New Zealand), Lyons (Australia)

Scorers: tries – O'Connor, Graham, Cleal, Brown, Ratier; goals – O'Connor (4)

Referee: J. Holdsworth (England)

Attendance: 12,409

GREAT BRITAIN v FRANCE

Two Tests against France provided the only 'serious business' for Great Britain in 1988–89, and Malcolm Reilly's team won their expected double. But, for British officials, more important than the wins was the growing confidence established in their team as they looked ahead to sterner challenges from New Zealand and Australia in the next two years.

Britain's controlled, confident 30–8 victory in Avignon was very satisfying for Reilly and all his men. Much was made after the win about the 'club spirit' in the British team, and the value of consistency in team selection building familiarity between players. With so few opportunities for the Great Britain team to play together, that build-up of consistency is vital.

Certainly, after their commanding display against France in that second Test, Great Britain looked in good shape. As well as that 'club spirit', the British have the priceless asset of a collection of brilliant individuals scattered throughout their side – all potential gamebreakers in tight situations. Martin Offiah, Phil Ford, Joe Lydon, Andy Gregory and Ellery Hanley head the list.

Great Britain also turned up a new attacking full-back of the highest quality in Alan Tait. Whether Tait has the defensive security and commanding presence of a fired-up Garry Jack, or a 1987–88 version of Steve Hampson, remains to be seen – but he surely can run, as was shown quite majestically on his way to a try down the right flank in Avignon. Tait had the distinction of being named Britain's most valuable player on his debut in the first Test at Wigan, and his pace and versatility seem set to make him a permanent fixture in the international squad for many years to come.

The Tests against France also provided the stage for the return of three 'prodigal sons' to the international arena, Shaun Edwards and Lee Crooks, after recovering from injuries that wrecked their 1988 tours, and Joe Lydon, suspension over and back to full fitness. Joe played both Tests like he really had something to prove – with gusto, determination and a level of vigour which was borderline stuff on several occasions.

Of course, France are the 'amateurs' of International Board Rugby League, and Great Britain must realise they cannot get carried away, no matter how many times they beat the French. In recent years both Australia and New Zealand have gone to France and won their Tests emphatically – something Great Britain had been unable to do until this year. Perhaps that's the sign that Britain's settled team and rising standards are taking effect. It certainly was no contest at Avignon's Parc des Sports on February 5, as the 'professionals' gave the 'amateurs' a hiding.

Alan Tait had an outstanding season for Widnes and proved himself one of the best attacking full-backs in the world. He had an especially good game against France at Wigan, his international debut, and his pace and versatility should secure for him a permanent place in the British squad for a long time to come.

Surprisingly, that optimism and the self-congratulatory mood apparent after Avignon was hardly evident in the first Test at Wigan two weeks before. There Great Britain did not have things their own way as France won many new friends, losing 10–26, but playing some vastly entertaining football along the way.

Britain seemed to find it hard to click into top gear – perhaps an inevitable result of the low key build-up to Tests against France in this country. As it turned out, the good form of the French, inspired by an excellent forward back-three of Buttignol, Verdes and Moliner, along with half-backs Palisses and Dumas, who got the better of Edwards and Gregory at Wigan, was probably just the motivation Great Britain needed for the return Test.

Ellery Hanley and his men knew they had to treat the Avignon match like a real Test, or risk embarrassment. In the event, France were back to square one, with a weak display which saw occasional flashes of brilliance (none better than a superlative try from captain Hugues Ratier) sandwiched between longer spells of infuriating ineptitude.

In short, Great Britain had them on toast after scoring 10 points before anybody had broken sweat. The captain, Hanley, played a major role, often taken for granted now since he has set such consistently high standards, and the mighty front-rowers Kevin Ward and Lee Crooks were just too big and powerful for the French pack to handle.

Watching Great Britain play France in 1989 is not unlike watching Australia play Great Britain in the early post-1982 encounters. No matter how much effort or entertaining football (to say nothing of the occasional spectacular try) one side produces, you just know the other team is going to win comfortably at the end of the day.

The relative physical power and tactical awareness of Britain and France is as different as one should expect between the products of an advancing professional League competition, and a largely amateur, low-pressure, often insecure League as is the case in France.

Compared to the no-mistakes professionalism of Great Britain, playing organised and methodical football, backed with an always steady kicking game, France looked just a collection of raw, albeit talented, individuals.

Despite lacking any of the big robust forwards of previous years (to say nothing of the absence of the man widely regarded as the best player in France, the Avignon scrum-half, Patrick Entat) the French really have improved their own standards and the discipline of their play. It's just unfortunate for them that Great Britain are steaming ahead, with the benefit of a tour behind them, and more 'together' than at any time in the past decade.

The better Great Britain get, the more difficult it is for France to keep pace and provide competitive opposition. But the French are trying manfully to keep moving upwards at international level, and the British can only be grateful for that as they look ahead to the visit of New Zealand this autumn.

Only two new players broke into the Great Britain side in 1988–89, Alan Tait and Salford's threequarter, Peter Williams. The consistency of personnel continues to be a major factor in Malcolm Reilly's planning, and Great Britain believe they are becoming a formidable force once again.

Wigan,
21 January

Great Britain 26 France 10

Great Britain: Tait (Widnes); Ford (Leeds), Loughlin (St Helens), Lydon (Wigan), Offiah (Widnes); Edwards (Wigan), Andy Gregory (Wigan); Ward (Castleford), Kevin Beardmore (Castleford), Waddell (Leeds), Mike Gregory (Warrington), Powell (Leeds), Hanley (Wigan)

Substitutes: Williams (Salford), Eyres (Widnes)

Scorers: tries – Edwards, Hanley, Ford, Offiah, Lydon; goals – Loughlin (3)

France: Fraisse (Le Pontet); Ratier (St Estève), Delaunay (St Estève), Eric Vergniol (Villeneuve), Criottier (Le Pontet); Palisses (St Estève), Dumas (St Gaudens); Rabot (Villeneuve), Valero (Pamiers), Pierre Aillères (Toulouse), Buttignol (Avignon), Verdes (Villeneuve), Moliner (Pamiers)

Substitutes: Tisseyre (Pamiers), Patrick Rocci (Le Pontet)

Scorers: tries – Moliner, Dumas; goal – Fraisse

Referee: G. McCallum (Australia)

Attendance: 8012

Avignon,
5 February

France 8 Great Britain 30

France: Frison (Toulouse); Ratier (St Estève), Delaunay (St Estève), Eric Vergniol (Villeneuve), Fraisse (Le Pontet); Palisses (St Estève), Dumas (St Gaudens); Rabot (Villeneuve), Valero (Pamiers), Pierre Aillères (Toulouse), Buttignol (Avignon), Verdes (Villeneuve), Moliner (Pamiers)

Substitutes: Tisseyre (Pamiers), Patrick Rocci (Le Pontet)

Scorers: tries – Dumas, Ratier

Great Britain: Tait (Widnes); Ford (Leeds), Williams (Salford), Lydon (Wigan), Offiah (Widnes); Edwards (Wigan), Andy Gregory (Wigan); Ward (Castleford), Kevin Beardmore (Castleford), Crooks (Leeds), Mike Gregory (Warrington), Powell (Leeds), Hanley (Wigan)

Substitutes: Hampson (Wigan), England (Castleford)

Scorers: tries – Ford (2), Edwards, Tait, Hanley, Williams; goals – Lydon (3)

Referee: G. McCallum (Australia)

Attendance: 6000

Headingley,
Leeds,
20 January

Great Britain Under-21 30 France Under-21 0

Great Britain Under-21: Bibb (Featherstone Rovers); Boothroyd (Castleford), Irwin (Castleford), Anderson (Castleford), Newlove (Featherstone Rovers); Richard Price (Hull), Southernwood (Castleford); Lucas (Wigan), Dermott (Wigan), Street (Leigh), Betts (Wigan), Gary Price (Wakefield Trinity), Gildart (Wigan)

Substitutes: Farrell (Huddersfield), Harmon (Warrington)

Scorers: tries – Gary Price (2), Richard Price, Irwin, Betts, Southernwood, Newlove; goal – Newlove

France Under-21: Fages (Pia); Chiron (Carpentras), Amar (Avignon), Despin (Villeneuve), Djebarni (Villeneuve); Garcia (St Estève), Delbert (Villeneuve); Rodriguez (Carcassonne), Guidicelli (Albi), Louazani (Carcassonne), Chamorin (St Estève), Cabestany (St Estève), Lafratte (St Gaudens)

Substitutes: Ascencio (Carcassonne), Durand (Avignon)

Referee: A. Sablayrolles (France)

Attendance: 3313

108

Paul Newlove of Featherstone Rovers, Great Britain's highly promising Under-21 centre or winger, is tackled in the international against France as Anthony Farrell of Huddersfield crashes on top of him.

Richard Price of Hull, Great Britain's stand-off in the Under-21 international against France at Carpentras, escapes the attentions of two French defenders.

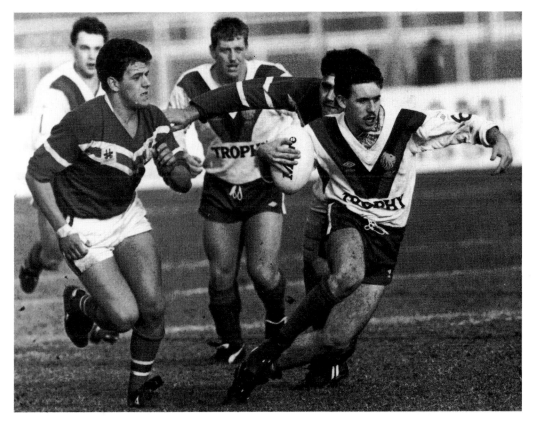

Carpentras,
4 February

France Under-21 16 Great Britain Under-21 8

France Under-21: Fages (Pia); Chiron (Carpentras), Daniel Vergniol (Villeneuve), Despin (Villeneuve), Reyre (Avignon); Garcia (St Estève), Mas (Avignon); Rodriguez (Carcassonne), Guidicelli (Albi), Roux (Carpentras), Jammes (Limoux), Cabestany (St Estève), Aubert (Le Pontet)

Substitutes: Durand (Avignon), Chamorin (St Estève)

Scorers: tries – Garcia (2), Mas; goals – Vergniol (2)

Great Britain Under-21: Bibb (Featherstone Rovers); Farrell (Huddersfield), Irwin (Castleford), Anderson (Castleford), Newlove (Featherstone Rovers); Richard Price (Hull), Southernwood (Castleford); Lucas (Wigan), Hill (Castleford), Street (Leigh), Betts (Wigan), Gary Price (Wakefield Trinity), Gildart (Wigan)

Substitutes: Lay (Hunslet), Harmon (Warrington)

Scorers: try – Hill; goals – Newlove (2)

Referee: D. Carter (England)

Attendance: 2500

Villeurbanne,
near Lyon,
11 March

France 'B' 62 Great Britain Amateurs 0

France 'B': Molitor (Le Pontet); Criottier (Le Pontet), Eric Vergniol (Villeneuve), Fraisse (Le Pontet), Chiron (Carpentras); Matter (Avignon), Entat (Avignon); Tisseyre (Pamiers), Khedimi (St Estève), Buttignol (Avignon), Saumitou (Villeneuve), Ruiz (Le Barcarès), Pech (Limoux)

Substitutes: Despin (Villeneuve), Tene (St Estève), Cabestany (St Estève)

Scorers: tries – Fraisse (3), Pech (2), Saumitou, Ruiz, Criottier, Tisseyre, Khedimi; goals – Vergniol (9), Fraisse (2)

Great Britain Amateurs: Honey (Thatto Heath); Sharp (Dudley Hill), Clarke (Kells), Alan Kelly (Egremont), Mercer (Heworth); Marsh (Leigh Miners), Pugsley (Leigh East); Williamson (Leigh Miners), Hankey (Rose Bridge), Thomason (Broughton Red Rose), Webb (Woolston), Dawson (Millom), Rawlinson (Dudley Hill)

Substitutes: Lumb (West Hull), Shaw (Dewsbury Albion), Gary Kelly (Millom)

Referee: A. Campbell (England)

Attendance: 2324

TWO

The Season in France 1988–89

Harry Edgar

French Rugby League is an acquired taste, not always palatable to the less enlightened Anglo-Saxon mentality. A bizarre mixture of sensitivity and sado-masochism, beautiful one minute and brutal the next, the life and times of the game in France have always been as unpredictable as their performances on the field of play.

The 1988–89 season did nothing to change that view. What was being admired as a thoroughly positive season on the road back to credibility was suddenly plunged into crisis again right at the end when Le Pontet, France's most progressive and successful club of recent years, threatened to withdraw from the Federation.

Le Pontet were incensed at refereeing decisions that went against them in both the Championship and Cup finals. The previous season's 'double' winners, and clearly the outstanding club side in France in 1988–89, the men from Provence, so well coached by the former international scrum-half, Marius Frattini, lost both their titles – the Championship to St Estève, 4–23, and the Cup to neighbours Avignon, 11–12. Much, much worse, however, was that Le Pontet also lost their tempers, their control, and the respect so widely held for them in French Rugby League.

The trouble flared in the 56th minute of the Championship final, played at Narbonne on 14 May. St Estève's Test centre, Guy Delaunay, was allowed to score a try after what appeared to be a clear knock-on and forward pass. Le Pontet blew up at referee Francis Desplats' decision, with their captain, Marc Palanques, losing all self-control. He was sent off, wouldn't go, aggressed the referee, and finally went to the locker-rooms after a ten minute interruption to the game.

A week later, Le Pontet defended the Lord Derby Cup against Avignon at Albi, and the build-up to that game was fraught with tension. Skipper Palanques and hooker Christian Macalli were suspended for their part in the Championship final unpleasantness, and Le Pontet threatened not to take the field without them.

Thankfully, the French Rugby League Federation did not give in to such blackmail, and, in their constant efforts to minimise violent behaviour, insisted that the suspended Le Pontet duo must not play.

The Cup final went ahead in scorching heat and, after leading 9–2 at half-time, Le Pontet again found their tempers rising when refereeing decisions went against them. Losing control of themselves inevitably led to Le Pontet losing control of the game, and Avignon, inspired by their scrum-half, Patrick Entat, won 12–11.

111

The return of the former international scrum-half, Guy Alard, provided a major boost for AS Carcassonne. Here Alard (*left*) challenges his half-back rival, Frédéric Bourrel, in the Aude regional derby between ASC and Limoux. Bourrel vied with St Gaudens's Gilles Dumas for the no. 7 jersey in the French national team, although it was Avignon's Patrick Entat who received fulsome praise as the best half-back in the country.

Worse was to follow in the dispute between Le Pontet and the French Federation, when the club then refused to take part in their scheduled European Cup challenge match against the British champions, Widnes. At two days notice, St Estève were called in to fill the breach and provide Widnes with opposition – albeit of a less than satisfactory standard. St Estève, coached by the national team mentor, Jacques Jorda, had got down to some heavy celebration partying in the aftermath of their Championship win, and, with some players away on holiday and others returned to Australia, were not prepared for a tough game against a side like Widnes. Playing at Arles, over 200 miles from the Perpignan suburb of St Estève, also meant that Jorda's team could not call on the always passionate home support French clubs enjoy.

The result, a 60–6 win for Widnes, did not really achieve anything for European Rugby League. The game was played, and in a good sporting spirit, but little else about it was worthy of note.

Had Widnes gone ahead with the two-legged contest with Le Pontet back in March, as originally scheduled, things might have been very different, and certainly English fans would have seen French club standards in a much more favourable light.

Meanwhile the Le Pontet fiasco grew out of all proportion when the Federation declared the club be suspended for twelve months. Le Pontet's response was to say they would join the Rugby Union Federation – the ultimate knife in the back for French *treizistes* who have suffered so cruelly from the antics of the Rugby Union over the years, particularly during the Second World War when League was banned totally.

With the smell of *treiziste* blood in their nostrils, Albert Ferrasse and the

Rugby Union Federation wasted no time in trying to capitalise on the disarray of the League and the Le Pontet club. It was publicly announced that all Rugby League clubs, players and officials would be welcomed into Rugby Union if they gave up the 13-a-side game and switched en masse to 15-a-side. Leading League officials were promised similar positions within the Union fraternity, if they wound up the League Federation.

Thankfully, the Union's enticement would be rejected, but the very audacity of the move emphasised just how blatantly the French ignore the rules and regulations of the Rugby Union International Board to which they belong. Earlier in the season stories of huge cash inducements being made to League stars to switch to the supposedly 'amateur' Rugby Union were rife. The prime targets were the scrum-half, Gilles Dumas, who said he had turned down a deal worth £50,000 to play for a Rugby Union club he would not name, Toulouse Olympique's full-back, Charles Frison, the national team captain, Hugues Ratier, and the exciting young threequarters, David Fraisse and Eric Vergniol. The French Rugby Union saw the latter duo as having the potential to be another Jo Maso or Patrick Sella, just two of the young players they had enticed from Rugby League in previous years.

The constant battle with a Rugby Union Federation that openly disregards that sport's rules on professionalism, and is in a position to buy whatever media coverage and government support it requires, hangs like a millstone around the neck of Rugby League in France. Until that fateful 56th minute in the Championship final, everything seemed to be going well for French Rugby League. Much work had gone into providing international links and competition for French players. The four-match tour undertaken by the Penrith club from Sydney provided a promotional boost, and a major upsurge in Franco-Australian relations, which had been somewhat strained since the 1986 Kangaroo tourists met such woeful organisation during the French section of their programme.

Penrith, led by coach Ron Willey, a long-time friend of French Rugby League, enjoyed marvellous hospitality in France. The Panthers won three of their four games – 16–6 v. Midi-Pyrénées at Toulouse, 40–4 v. Le Pontet, and 23–16 v. a French national selection at Perpignan. Their one defeat was against a L'Aude selection at Carcassonne.

The Penrith visit was followed by a mini-tour to England undertaken by a French national squad including many young newcomers. Captained by their winger, Hugues Ratier, France used the English tour to expose their players to both professional opposition and the experience of touring.

In their first game France beat Warrington 29–6 in a stunning exhibition of all that is best in French Rugby League. So often, watching a French team flit from sheer magic to almost juvenile ineptitude, one would sigh and think 'if only, one day, all those vital passes were held instead of being dropped or intercepted . . . somebody's going to get a hammering.' At Wilderspool they did, and the French were probably more surprised than anybody else that, for once, their luck and their nerve held.

Jorda's team lost their other two tour games – against a determined and tough Cumbria county team at Whitehaven, 13–18, and against Halifax, 18–24, after a free-flowing game full of sparkling rugby.

Pierre Montgaillard (XIII Catalan) in possession and on the attack against Avignon in a French championship match at Perpignan. It was a disappointing season for the Catalans. Montgaillard had his personal disappointments, too, losing his place in the national team to Avignon's outstanding captain, Thierry Buttignol, the very defender who blocks his path in this picture.

The experience gained was most useful for Jacques Jorda and his players. The game in France depends, so much, on results at international level, both for its credibility in the eyes of the public and its level of financial support from the government. In this way, League always suffers in comparison with Rugby Union. Now that New Zealand and Great Britain have followed Australia's lead in Rugby League, it is becoming almost impossible for France to win any Test matches, even at home. In Rugby Union, no matter how poor the opposition might be, a French victory always enhances the positive aspects of the game. Standards are so much higher in world Rugby League, and just to be able to compete is a credit to a French team which is the product of a less than ideal club championship.

But French League is improving. The work put in at national team level by, first, Tas Baitieri, and now Jorda and Louis Bonnery, has had a positive effect. When the opposition is anything less than extremely well organised and highly motivated, France can compete very well. They did this in the Test at Wigan last season, when only that vital lack of 'professionalism' and finishing power prevented them going close to victory in a game most pre-match tipsters had predicted would be a rout for Great Britain.

What cannot be denied about French Rugby League is that it continues to produce a succession of very talented young players. The difficulty – some might say tragedy – is the failure to harness this talent, and give it the environment in which to achieve its full potential at senior club level, and, thereby, senior international level.

It was an eventful season for the French captain, Hugues Ratier. He led France on their mini tour of England and in both Test matches against Great Britain, as well as gaining selection for the Rest of the World XIII at Headingley. Ratier left the unhappy Lézignan club after many seasons' proud service, to join Jacques Jorda's St Estève team. Ratier finished the campaign as the championship's top try-scorer, and captained St Estève to the title.

So many excellent young players just drop out of Rugby League in France and are never heard of again. Some go to Rugby Union, some play 'social' League in the lower divisions of the French Championship, and others quit altogether.

At youth levels, French teams have always held their own against British counterparts. They did in 1988–89. The French Juniors (aged 20 and under) came back against all the odds to beat Great Britain Under-21s at Carpentras, 16–8, after suffering an overwhelming 0–30 defeat at Headingley, in which it looked like a clear case of men against boys, professionals against amateurs.

The same French side won an excellent double against the BARLA Under-19s, reputedly the strongest for years, with many 'signed' players maintaining their amateur status in order to represent Great Britain.

But, at senior level, the more Great Britain improves its standards, the more difficult it is for France to compete. Sadly, most French observers outside the immediate confines of their national squad and coaching scheme, just don't realise how much better Great Britain are becoming and how tough that makes life for the French players.

However, the theory that France were now on a level where they could only compete with BARLA, and not the professionals, was totally refuted when France B annihilated the Great Britain Amateurs 62–0 at Villeurbanne in March.

That game was notable for the return to the tricolour jersey of their scrum-half, Patrick Entat, his first national selection during the Test regime of Jorda, Bonnery and manager Jean Panno. For two years, Entat has been at logger-heads with the national selectors, and both Gilles Dumas and Frederic Bourrel have been preferred at scrum-half. But the brilliant form of the Avignon player could not be ignored, and his agreement to play for France B was seen as an olive branch on the way back to the Test team to play New Zealand in the autumn.

Entat was voted France's player of the season – his glory complete when he inspired Avignon to win the Lord Derby Cup. The other outstanding performers in the 1988–89 Championship were John Maguirre, Le Pontet's Australian centre, Thierry Bernabé, the veteran Le Pontet former international loose forward or hooker, Pierre Aillères, Toulouse Olympique's mighty front-rower, and Eric Vergniol, Villeneuve's exciting young centre.

The club competition had been dominated by Le Pontet, until those final tragic moments of mayhem in the Championship final. They finished top of the first division's Poule A and, in the play-offs, beat Villeneuve 31–0 and XIII Catalan 5–4 to reach that ill-fated final against St Estève.

As for St Estève, the second Championship title in their history was a popular win. Jacques Jorda had them playing attractive open rugby, with the same kind of discipline he has instilled into the national team. On their way to the final, St Estève beat Carcassonne 22–10, then Limoux 17–10 in the semi-final.

Certainly Le Pontet and St Estève were clearly regarded as the best club teams in France, with the always solid Avignon and Toulouse Olympique not far behind. XIII Catalan lost their crown of invincibility, and, despite their professionalism in so many areas, an inability to curb the violent behaviour of some of their players remains a curse of the Catalans, and of the French Federation as a whole.

AS Carcassonne, the giants of the French game in the glory days soon after the Second World War, took some strides back to former greatness after several lean years. The return of the former international scrum-half, Guy Alard, gave the 'Canaries' direction, and ASC remains one of France's most ambitious and most respected clubs.

The saddest story was the demise of the Lézignan club, one of French Rugby League's founding pioneers. Bedevilled by internal politics that led to a massive player walkout at the start of the season, Lézignan had a disastrous season, ending in relegation to Poule B. They will be replaced by promoted Pamiers, who set new standards in Poule B, largely as a result of having three outstanding Test players in their ranks, Marc Tisseyre, Jacques Moliner and Thierry Valero (the latter two recruits from Lézignan!).

The leading points scorer in France was Le Pontet's David Fraisse, with 212 points from 21 tries and 64 goals. Behind him came Eric Vergniol (Villeneuve) with 206 points, Michel Roses (St Estève) with 201 points and Gilles Dumas

116

(St Gaudens) with 149 points. The top try-scorer was the St Estève winger and Test captain, Hugues Ratier, with twenty-four.

After such a good season, the tragedy of those moments of madness in the Championship final, followed by the Le Pontet saga, were hard to take for French Rugby League. Their officials seem to have perfected the fine art of shooting themselves in the foot, just when sunlight appears on the horizon.

If Le Pontet are lost to Rugby League the gap in the French Federation will be enormous. Not only did the club contest both major finals, and provide a host of players for national teams, but their reserves also won both the second division Championship and the Coupe Fédérale, while their Juniors were close runners-up to the outstanding Villeneuve colts in their national Championship.

Perhaps part of the attraction of French Rugby League is its glorious uncertainty – but one often wonders just how many more self-inflicted wounds it can take, especially when the spectre of Monsieur Ferrasse and his cohorts hovers so menacingly in the background, eager to kill the beast at the earliest opportunity.

The charismatic Jacques Jorda celebrates St Estève's victory in the championship final at Narbonne. There is a strong possibility that Jorda will become the new coach of XIII Catalan, working alongside the former Test scrum-half, Yvan Grésèque, as 'directeur sportif'.

THREE

The Season in Australia 1989

David Middleton

Building on the unqualified success and public support of the 1988 season, Australian Rugby League reached even greater heights in 1989. Starting with a multi-million dollar advertising campaign, featuring Tina Turner, the league reached out and captivated a new audience for both the Panasonic Cup and the Winfield Cup. Crowds at Winfield Cup fixtures surpassed the record figures of 1988, despite the wettest season in the history of the game in Australia.

The burgeoning support proved that the quality of the product justified the advertising outlay. Interest in the game crossed new frontiers. The March Panasonic Cup match in Perth, Western Australia, attracted more than 24,000 paying spectators and television networking brought the game into hundreds of thousands of homes for the first time. The selling power of Rugby League skyrocketed. When Channel Ten, the station which has covered the Winfield Cup and the Panasonic Cup for the past six years, eventually secured the television rights for the next three years they paid $42 million – a record for television sport in Australia – surpassing even the Olympic Games coverage. Indeed, the battle of the networks for the exclusive television rights was the toughest off-field contest of the year. The three-year deal will include all State of Origin telecasts, the Winfield Cup, the Panasonic Cup and all Test matches. In 1989, Channel Ten made historic live broadcasts from Parkes, Perth, Townsville and other country centres as they helped the league to broaden the spread of the game.

The trend towards a national competition grew stronger after the success of the Perth match. And the real possibility of a Western Australian team entering the Sydney competition within five years prompted much discussion.

The strength of the game in Queensland, too, became more and more apparent as the season unfolded. The Panasonic Cup match in Townsville, North Queensland, reinforced the tremendous interest in the game there and also prompted talk of basing a Winfield Cup team in the north. The success of Queensland in the State of Origin and of Brisbane in the Winfield and Panasonic Cups highlighted the talent available in that state. With most of Queensland behind the team and the ability to draw on the sponsorship resources of a whole state, Brisbane became an instant force in premiership calculations.

This was highlighted in the Panasonic Cup final when a crowd of 16,000 urged on the financial lightweights Illawarra in a tremendous game against the Brisbane Broncos, regarded by southern supporters as bitter rivals. When Illawarra failed at the final hurdle, Brisbane were cockahoop. Each trip to Sydney became a mini-State of Origin match for the Broncos, and the 'us against the world' syndrome gave them a significant psychological boost.

The league's $4.5 million advertising deal with the Queen of Rock and Roll, Tina Turner, was undoubtedly the sporting marketing coup of the decade. The sight of Tina strutting and pouting to the hit song *What You Get is What You See* with images of the bright young faces of the Winfield Cup players on television throughout the country was the most flamboyant marketing strategy ever attempted by a sport in Australia. Turner filmed the commercial in London with Aussie League players Cliff Lyons and Gavin Miller at Fulham's ground and at Tottenham Hotspur's White Hart Lane stadium in December 1988.

John Ferguson, NSW's winger, races away in the third State of Origin match, won by Queensland 36–16.

If that was one of the brightest moments for Rugby League in 1989, the darkest and saddest came a few weeks before the advertising campaign was launched. A shocking car accident after a St George club social cricket match claimed the life of the rising young star Geoff Selby and left two other first-graders, Shaun O'Bryan and Peter Gentle, in hospital. As a schoolboy Selby had earlier toured England with James Cook High School, under the coaching of Hull's Australian mentor, Brian Smith.

News of Parramatta champion Peter Sterling's departure to Headingley was confirmed early in the season. A testimonial year was held in honour of the player, rated one of the best half-backs of all time, and his loss will be a body blow to the Parramatta club. His unavailability for representative selection was similarly hard-felt by New South Wales, who went down in the State of Origin series for the third successive year.

Another feature of the 1989 season was the impact of British players on the Australian game: Andy Gregory and Steve Hampson (Illawarra), Shaun Edwards and Andy Currier (Balmain), Ellery Hanley, Garry Schofield and Kelvin Skerrett (Wests), Martin Offiah and Joe Lydon (Easts), Hugh Waddell (Manly), and Graham Steadman (Gold Coast) were all welcome additions to their clubs and were regular first-graders. Additionally, David McCann (Canterbury), Paul Vannet (Cronulla), Des Foy (Newcastle), Bernard Dwyer (Manly) and Tracey Lazenby (Penrith) were other Englishmen to find a home in Sydney.

THE PANASONIC CUP

The rich Panasonic Cup made astonishing inroads into new areas in 1989, opening the way for possible future expansion on a national scale in Australia. The organisers took Cup matches as far afield as Perth (5000 km west of Sydney) and Townsville (2500 km north of Sydney) and were overwhelmed by the public's excited reaction, especially in Perth.

The Perth match was between Balmain, the 1988 Grand Finalists and Panasonic Cup runners-up, and Parramatta, four times premiers in the 1980s. The Western Australian League staged a most efficient promotion campaign to publicise the biggest event in their history, flying both teams over well before the match to run coaching clinics and conduct media interviews.

A crowd of 24,643 at the WACA ground was a record for paying spectators at the famous cricket arena and it was reported that NSWRL officials were amazed at the size of the crowd but more so at the locals' affinity with the Sydney clubs. Supporters in Balmain and Parramatta jerseys were in abundance and the atmosphere was electric. Then Parramatta produced the first shock of the 1989 Cup by winning 22–12 after trailing 0–12, and Balmain made an early exit after appearing in the previous four Panasonic finals.

The competition had kicked off a week earlier in the western NSW town of Parkes (population 9500), when the glamorous Canberra and Brisbane teams clashed. A mighty crowd of 9862 converged on the Pioneer Oval from outlying districts and witnessed a game of the highest standard. Brisbane won 18–13 after Canberra had dominated for the first two quarters.

After those memorable opening matches, the standard of play in the Cup, the support and the excitement, grew and grew. In May the Cup 'roadshow' picked up and went north to the booming North Queensland tourist centre of Townsville for a quarter-final match between Parramatta and Brisbane. The record crowd of more than 16,000 not only emphasised the massive support for Rugby League in the north, but also that the whole state of Queensland was behind the Brisbane Broncos. After the match there was speculation that a second Queensland team, based in the north, could enter a 'national' Winfield Cup within five years.

The Broncos really cut loose in that match, scoring eight tries to one, with the indomitable Wally Lewis scoring a hat-trick. That win put them into a semi-final play-off with South Sydney, who at the time were sharing the

Winfield Cup lead with Brisbane. That match was played in sub-zero temperatures in the one-time gold-mining town of Bathurst, in western NSW. Again a record crowd watched the game. More than 10,000 packed into Carrington Park, to watch Lewis and his Broncos produce more magic to beat Souths 24–4 in a spirited encounter.

Garry Jack, NSW's full-back, kicks past Queensland's Alan McIndoe and Walters. All three State of Origin matches were won by Queensland.

In the other half of the competition draw Illawarra were writing their own fairytale with wins over Wests, Cronulla and Norths to find their way to an historic Cup final showdown with Brisbane. The Steelers had caused the shock of the competition with an astounding 40–0 thrashing of the glamour Cronulla club. At the time Illawarra had not won a match in the Winfield Cup, but with the Great Britain imports, Andy Gregory and Steve Hampson, watching from the sidelines, the team gelled like never before. The Wigan pair, who later became the first players to take part in the Challenge Cup final and the Panasonic Cup final in the same year, inspired the Steelers to great deeds.

Against Cronulla the team could do no wrong, but their semi-final against Norths was another story. The team looked down and out as they trailed Norths with only minutes to play before their talented young hooker, Dean Schifilliti, beat three Norths defenders to a rolling ball and his try levelled the scores at 12–12. But under Cup rules, if the scores and the number of tries

121

scored are level, then the winner is decided on a penalty countback. Norths and Canterbury (who were beaten in a quarter-final by Souths) could consider themselves hard done by to bow out in this manner. The penalty countback (incidentally to be reviewed before the start of the 1990 season) is a dubious rule because a referee can deprive a team of a penalty by allowing an advantage – and under Cup rules that could cost them the game.

Anyway, Illawarra, having won nothing in their eight seasons in the Sydney premiership, advanced to the final – and the biggest game in their history. On the Winfield Cup ladder they were a distant last. The Brisbane Broncos, facing them, were boosted by seven internationals and three State of Origin representatives. If ever there was a David and Goliath contest this was it. Support for Illawarra at the Parramatta stadium was overwhelming. It became a mini-State of Origin clash and the Broncos were the arch enemy. When Brisbane raced to a 16–0 lead after twenty-three minutes they were greeted by a volley of abuse.

The unprecedented support for Illawarra, the team from the south coast town of Wollongong, galvanised them into action. A try from an Andy Gregory kick inspired the comeback. Then their outstanding wing prospect, Rod Wishart, scored a thrilling try from an intercept and the Steelers trailed 12–16 at half-time. Illawarra dominated possession in the third quarter as Brisbane continued to repel them. A minute from three-quarter time, Wishart kicked a penalty under enormous pressure from the sideline after Gregory was felled off the ball.

It set up a monumental final quarter as both teams extended themselves fully. The Test centre, Peter Jackson, put on a try for Gene Miles minutes from full-time and the conversion by the series superstar-award winner, Terry Matterson, put Brisbane ahead 22–14 and the Broncos looked certain winners. But they didn't count on another Illawarra comeback, when Steve Hampson dummied to his outside man and scored wide out. Wishart's conversion, again from the sideline reduced the deficit to 20–22 with a minute to play. Despite their best efforts to throw the ball wide from the kick-off, play broke down and Brisbane had the title. It was a magnificent finale to a series of compelling football action.

THE WINFIELD CUP

Not even the wettest Rugby League season in history could dampen the enthusiasm of supporters or players in the hardest fought Sydney premiership yet. The league's advertising blurb – 'Now the big game's even bigger' – was true in every sense. The second year of the expanded competition, which included Newcastle, the Gold Coast and Brisbane for the first time in 1988, attracted unprecedented interest through the gates as the sixteen teams battled for the Winfield Cup. The 'big-three' teams – Souths, Brisbane and Canberra – continued to fight off challengers as the semi-finals approached. Souths confounded the critics to hold the competition lead at the half-way mark after their coach, George Piggins, watched his team fall around him through injury.

Players like Ian Roberts, Les Davidson and David Boyle spent long periods on the sidelines but the spirit of the famous Red and Greens shone through and they remained unbeaten for eleven weeks up to late June.

The emergence of a band of dedicated rookies helped ease Souths through a crisis, and while props Mark Lyons and Darren Brown, and the seventeen-year-old hooker, Jim Serdaris, may not yet be household names, they did their club proud in trying circumstances. The half-back combination of Craig Coleman and Phil Blake, who honed their talents in Britain during the Australian off-season, were the architects of much of Souths' work. Brisbane, short-priced favourites for the crown, were in search of the Mid-week Cup and Premiership double – a feat performed only by Easts in 1975 and Parramatta in 1986. And there were few prepared to bet against the Broncos, with the nucleus of the Queensland side performing with distinction each week. In their ranks were the Origin players Michael Hancock, Tony Currie, Wally Lewis, Allan Langer, Gene Miles, Sam Backo, Kerrod Walters and Chris Johns (NSW), making them one of the competition's most feared outfits.

The leg fracture which Langer sustained in the second State of Origin match robbed him of a Test half-back jersey in New Zealand and almost certainly stopped him taking out a string of player-of-the-year awards. Until his injury Langer was one of the most dominating players in the Australian game.

Canberra, buoyed up by a marvellous home ground record and a team of all the talents, were the dark horses for the premiership in the lead-up to the finals. Successive wins over the Gold Coast, Canterbury, Illawarra, St George, Parramatta and Brisbane at their Seiffert Oval headquarters had them going well for a place in the top three. A backline which boasted the internationals Mal Meninga, Gary Belcher and John Ferguson, as well as such talents as Laurie Daley, Ivan Henjak and Chris O'Sullivan, was one of the most powerful and free-flowing in the competition.

Surprisingly, the 1988 heavyweights, Balmain and Canterbury, had faded from the picture after a mid-season slump that could have been attributed to their big forwards becoming bogged down by the atrocious surfaces they had to contend with each week. Canterbury slumped to losses against St George, Canberra, Souths and Newcastle before the most humiliating defeat of all – a 4–38 hammering by the improving Penrith side in May. Basing their game on a formula of tough and aggressive football, Penrith were emerging as genuine challengers despite a couple of below par performances. With experienced campaigners Royce Simmons, Chris Mortimer, Peter Kelly and Geoff Gerard adding their knowhow to a skilful band of younger players such as Greg Alexander, John Cartwright, Mark Geyer, Graeme Bradley and Colin Van der Voort, the Panthers looked to be getting the blend just right.

Balmain, meanwhile, were rocked by injuries and suspensions and never asserted the authority of their 1988 campaign. Their talented Kiwi Test half-back, Gary Freeman, was cited on a charge of gouging and suspended for twelve weeks early in the season and the Great Britain player, Shaun Edwards, also spent two weeks suspended after being found guilty of a high tackle in only his second match on Aussie soil. Wayne Pearce (broken thumb) and Garry Jack (broken arm) were sidelined early in the year and Jack, in particular, took a long time to regain his confidence and form.

At Newcastle, the amazing crowd support of 1988 continued in 1989, as they became the most popular team in the competition. And performances on the field improved too. Their record at their International Sports Centre headquarters was impeccable although they struggled for consistency away from home. Mark Sargent, Michael Hagan and Gary Wurth were the newcomers helping to make things happen for the Knights. Cronulla lacked the consistency of their 1988 season, the year they won their first minor premiership title, but they were still well placed for a tilt at the semi-finals as the second half of the competition progressed. The big name players, Gavin Miller, Andrew Ettingshausen and Mark McGaw, were providing the skills that had the Sharks hovering among the top five teams.

The major disappointments for 1989 were the glamour clubs, Easts and Manly. Manly, the 1987 premiers, were nowhere to be sighted as the teams rounded the competition's half-way mark and confidence and team morale was at a low ebb. The Sea Eagles were overflowing with class. Dale Shearer, Michael O'Connor, Darrell Williams, Des Hasler, Cliff Lyons, Paul Vautin, Noel Cleal and Phil Daley were expected to lead a Manly charge to the semi-finals, but under the coaching of the former Kangaroo five-eighth, Alan Thompson, Manly faltered badly. The administration restricted off-season buying to two schoolboy representatives and the Great Britain prop, Hugh Waddell; despite missing out on Kevin Ward for a third stint, the personnel should have been adequate.

Easts, on the other hand, 'bought big' in the off season. Paul Mares and Mick Delroy from Parramatta, Sandy Campbell from Canterbury, the Rugby Union international Michael Cook, and the British stars, Joe Lydon and Martin Offiah, cost the Roosters a lot of money but by the time Lydon and Offiah arrived in May Easts were already amongst the also-rans. They had started the season with great promise with a 14–0 win over Souths, but discipline and commitment soon fell by the wayside, along with the fortunes of the team.

Parramatta were another team to run hot and cold, although with players of the calibre of Peter Sterling, Brett Kenny and Eric Grothe in their side they were always going to be a threat. The encouraging debut in Rugby League of the former Wallaby full-back, Andrew Leeds, was a bright part of the Eels' season. After starting the year with a flurry – they won their first four matches – the Eels dropped their next three, bringing themselves right back to the field.

St George performed way above expectations to enter into semi-final calculations midway through the season. A youth development programme at the club, and the coaching of the former international, Craig Young, paid rich dividends for the famous Dragons and names like Brad Mackay, Shane Kelly, Paul Osborne and Jason Hoogerwerf were beginning to emerge as top-line first-grade players. Mackay even earned his stripes as a replacement for New South Wales in the final two State of Origin matches.

After again promising so much in the off-season build-up North Sydney failed to deliver. On their day they showed the ability to match strides with the best in the competition – their 34–18 hiding of Parramatta was proof of that – but their day arrived all too rarely. They had some of the best players in the business on their books but as has been proved by years of failed campaigns,

Michael Hancock, Queensland's teenage winger, is developing into a top-class player and was picked for Australia's squad to tour New Zealand. Here, in the third State of Origin match, he is tackled from behind and his way forward is blocked by NSW's Chris Johns.

there is a stigma about the red and black jumper of North Sydney which is a sizable barrier to success.

The fledgling club, Gold Coast, earned respect with victories over Easts, Wests and Newcastle and some courageous displays which took them within an ace of victory over Canterbury and St George. The Featherstone five-eighth, Graham Steadman, added a new attacking dimension to the Giants' backline when he arrived in Australia in late May.

The western Sydney satellite city of Campbelltown was abuzz with Ellery Hanley fever when the Great Britain captain kicked off his stint with Western Suburbs on 14 May. Orana Park had never experienced such hype and expectation. Hanley, along with fellow British players, Garry Schofield and Kelvin Skerrett, lifted crowds and team performances.

The fight and determination in the Illawarra team, after their heart-breaking Panasonic Cup final loss to Brisbane, made it difficult to understand how the Wollongong club could be trailing the Winfield Cup field with just one win at the competition's half-way mark. However, against Brisbane they showed their true capabilities and the introduction of Andy Gregory and Steve Hampson to the club established a winning attitude. In the past the Steelers had been too ready to live with defeat, but Gregory and Hampson made losing unacceptable and the improvement in the team, and in youngsters such as Rod Wishart and Brett Rodwell in particular, was noticeable after their arrival.

125

First
State of Origin,
Lang Park,
Brisbane,
23 May

Queensland 36, New South Wales 6

Queensland produced the most stunning display in the history of State of Origin matches to obliterate the Blues 36–6 in the opening match of the series at Brisbane's Lang Park. All the hype and expectation of the New South Wales line-up, coached by Jack Gibson, was wiped out in eighty minutes of precision teamwork and spectacular ball movement. Never has either State been given such a comprehensive thrashing in Origin football, and Queensland's seven try to one advantage was as much indicative of their magnificence as New South Wales's ineptitude.

The vastly inexperienced New South Wales outfit managed to hold Queensland for the tension-packed opening of the match but when that diminutive marvel, Allan Langer, pressed the go-button midway through the first half, the tries came in a deluge. Langer opted to take a penalty tap inside New South Wales's quarter. He ran across field and threw a long floating pass to his winger, Alan McIndoe, who broke the deadlock in a twenty-metre dash to the try-line. If that try exposed New South Wales, the following six laid their defences bare.

There wasn't a weak link in the Queensland side. Up front the Maroons' pack asserted their authority early and it was never questioned by the Blues' forwards, who failed to take the game to the opposition. The big prop, Martin Bella, took the honours in the forwards for Queensland, and emerged with the press writers' man-of-the-match award in a close vote from Langer.

Mal Meninga made a triumphant return to the State of Origin arena after battling for almost two years with a broken arm that refused to heal. He scored two tries and landed four goals to put him back on top of the State of Origin points scorers.

Queensland: Belcher; McIndoe, Currie, Meninga, Hancock; Lewis (capt.), Langer; Bella, Walters, Stains, Vautin, Miles, Lindner

Substitutes: Shearer for McIndoe and Coyne for Miles after 70 minutes, Hagan for Vautin after 74 minutes, Gillmeister for Walters (10 minutes head bin)

Scorers: tries – Hancock (2), Meninga (2), McIndoe, Langer, Lindner; goals – Meninga (4)

New South Wales: Jack; Johns, Farrar, Daley, Ferguson; Lamb, Hasler; Cartwright, Fenech, Dunn, Miller (capt.) Sironen, Clyde

Substitutes: Lazarus for Cartwright, Alexander for Clyde, Ettingshausen for Farrar all after 50 minutes, Mortimer for Sironen after 60 minutes

Scorers: try – Ettingshausen; goal – Daley

Referee: M. Stone (NSW)

Attendance: 32,000

126

Second State of Origin, Sydney Football Stadium, 14 June

New South Wales 12, Queensland 16

With one marvellous sleight of hand, Wally Lewis steered Queensland to a series victory over New South Wales at the Sydney Football Stadium. Facing a rejuvenated New South Wales line-up before a capacity crowd, the Queenslanders were seriously extended for the only time in the series.

With his team falling around him, Lewis took the game by the scruff of the neck midway through the second half with a try of power, pace and precision thinking. From a New South Wales error, the replacement half-back, Michael Hagan, scooped up the ball and sent it on to Lewis, thirty metres from the Blues' line. The defence converged on Lewis, but he outpaced the cover, beat Laurie Daley's tackle from behind and carried the full-back, Garry Jack, over the try-line with him. It was a try that not only changed the fortunes of the game but won the series for Queensland for an historic sixth time.

Dale Shearer looks for support in the third State of Origin match. Wally Lewis is on the right. Shearer was included in the Australian squad for New Zealand and was picked on the wing for the first Test in Christchurch.

Heroically, Queensland held their narrow lead with Langer (broken ankle), Lindner (cheekbone and ankle), Meninga (cheekbone), Vautin (elbow) and Hancock (shoulder) all off the field, playing the last five minutes a man short after using all four replacements. It took a champion team to win against such adversity and against a New South Wales team who seemed to have learned from many of their mistakes in the first game.

127

There were plenty of New South Wales stars. Bradley Clyde, Bruce McGuire, Greg Alexander, Peter Kelly, Gavin Miller, Chris Johns and Mario Fenech did nothing to tarnish their reputations despite the loss. The difference between the sides was undoubtedly Lewis, the man who burst into the State of Origin matches nine years ago and who has contributed greatly to the success of the series throughout the 1980s.

Queensland: Belcher; McIndoe, Currie, Meninga, Hancock; Lewis (capt.), Langer; Backo, Walters, Bella, Vautin, Miles, Lindner

Substitutes: Hagan for Langer after 19 minutes, Shearer for Meninga after 29 minutes, Gillmeister for Vautin at half-time, Coyne for Hancock after 57 minutes

Scorers: tries – Hancock, Walters, Lewis; goals – Meninga, Belcher

New South Wales: Jack; Ferguson, Ettingshausen, Daley, Johns; Mortimer, Alexander; Kelly, Fenech, Dunn, McGuire, Miller (capt.), Clyde

Substitutes: Hasler for Mortimer, Cartwright for Kelly, Mackay for Daley all after 59 minutes, Wilson for Dunn after 70 minutes

Scorers: tries – Daley, Johns; goals – Alexander (2)

Referee: D. Manson (Queensland)

Attendance: 40,000 (capacity)

Third
State of Origin,
Lang Park,
Brisbane,
28 June

Queensland 36, New South Wales 16
'One of the greatest teams of all time'. That was the tag given to Queensland after they had swept up the series with a commanding 36–16 victory before another sell-out crowd. Despite holding a 2–0 lead in the three matches, Queensland's supporters turned out in force to acclaim their team. What they saw was an outpouring of class and teamwork that blew New South Wales off Lang Park.

After trailing at half-time, Queensland finished up scoring seven tries to extend their winning sequence in official series competition to eight matches. Emerging from their team was a crop of new stars to carry Queensland's fortunes into the 1990s. Among them were players such as the hooker, Kerrod Walters, who won the man-of-the-match award and was unofficially named player-of-the-series by the ARL chairman, Ken Arthurson. A year ago Walters languished in reserve grade for the Brisbane Broncos, behind Test rake Greg Conescu. But his form in 1989 thrust him ahead of the veteran Conescu and he didn't look back. His darting forays from dummy-half caught the Blues by surprise on numerous occasions and he was an outstanding contender for the Australian hooking role in New Zealand.

The teenage winger, Michael Hancock, developed into a top-class player, making the most of every opportunity. He showed genuine pace and the ability to step off either foot. He finished his first Origin series with four tries. Easing them into the State of Origin cauldron was a core of experience and solidity that has provided the backbone of Queensland teams in recent seasons. Skipper Wally Lewis and centre Mal Meninga both played in the first State of Origin match in 1980. Gene Miles, Dale Shearer, Paul Vautin and Gary Belcher have been regular performers over a number of years.

Wally Lewis, Australia's outstanding captain, was picked to lead the Australian squad to New Zealand after another great State of Origin series.

Queensland: Belcher; McIndoe, Currie, Shearer, Hancock; Lewis (capt.), Hagan; Backo, Walters, Bella, Miles, Stains, Vautin

Substitutes: Jackson for Currie after 68 minutes, Coyne for Miles and Gillmeister for Kerrod Walters both after 70 minutes, Kevin Walters for Lewis after 72 minutes

Scorers: tries – Shearer (2), McIndoe, Hancock, Kerrod Walters, Belcher, Currie; goals – Shearer (4)

New South Wales: Jack; Ferguson, Johns, Johnston, O'Connor; Hasler, Alexander; McGuire, Trewhella, Kelly, Miller (capt.), Geyer, Clyde

Substitutes: Matterson for Geyer after 50 minutes, Cartwright for Kelly and Blake for Jack both after 62 minutes, Wilson for Trewhella after 68 minutes

Referee: G. McCallum (New South Wales)

Attendance: 33,000 (capacity)

The Australian squad for the three-week, six-match tour of New Zealand was announced after the State of Origin matches. It was:

Managers: Kevin Brasch, Peter Moore
Coach: Bob Fulton
Medical officer: Keith Woodhead
Trainers: Bryan Hider, Brian Hollis, John Lewis.

Team:
Greg Alexander (Penrith & NSW)
Sam Backo (Brisbane & Queensland)
Gary Belcher (Canberra & Queensland)
Martin Bella (Norths & Queensland)
Bradley Clyde (Canberra & NSW)
Tony Currie (Brisbane & Queensland)
Michael Hancock (Brisbane & Queensland)
Des Hasler (Manly & NSW)
Peter Jackson (Brisbane & Queensland)
Wally Lewis (capt.) (Brisbane & Queensland)
Bruce McGuire (Balmain & NSW)
Mal Meninga (Canberra & Queensland)
Michael O'Connor (Manly & NSW)
Steve Roach (Balmain & NSW)
Dale Shearer (Manly & Queensland)
Paul Sironen (Balmain & NSW)
Dan Stains (Cronulla & Queensland)
David Trewhella (Easts & NSW)
Paul Vautin (Manly & Queensland)
Kerrod Walters (Brisbane & Queensland)

It was no surprise that Queensland players figured in the team in record proportions. The Maroons' domination of the 1989 State of Origin series resulted in no fewer than twelve of their number being selected for the squad. And regular Australian team members, such as Gene Miles, Allan Langer and Bob Lindner, would also have been automatic selections had not injuries ruled them out of contention in the lead-up to the tour. The only omission from the winning Queensland team was the winger, Alan McIndoe, who had picked up two tries, and could consider himself unlucky not to go.

The big Balmain prop, Steve Roach, was the only player included in the squad who didn't play in the Origin series, but his vast international experience and his performance for Australia in the 1988 World Cup final win over New Zealand stood him in good stead. It was strongly rumoured that it was the new national coach, Bob Fulton, who favoured Roach, along with the discarded New South Wales forward, Paul Sironen, as well as Michael O'Connor, Peter Jackson and Sam Backo. The winger Michael Hancock and the forwards

Dan Stains, Bruce McGuire, David Trewhella, Kerrod Walters and Bradley Clyde all earned their first international jerseys.

After the squad's arrival in New Zealand, nine Queenslanders earned selection for the first Test at Christchurch. The team was: Belcher; Hancock, Currie, Meninga, Shearer; Lewis (capt.), Alexander (NSW); Backo, Walters, Roach (NSW), Sironen (NSW), Clyde (NSW), Vautin.

NSW's Des Hasler is held by Michael Hancock (*left*) and Tony Currie in the third State of Origin match in Brisbane.

After three seasons waiting in the wings, the Queensland full-back, Gary Belcher, finally wrested the Australian jersey from the former incumbent, Garry Jack. Jack's form slumped alarmingly throughout 1989 after he broke his arm early in the season. While the New South Wales selectors stuck by him throughout the Origin series, the national selectors could not deny the claims of Belcher, whose form in those matches was consistently excellent.

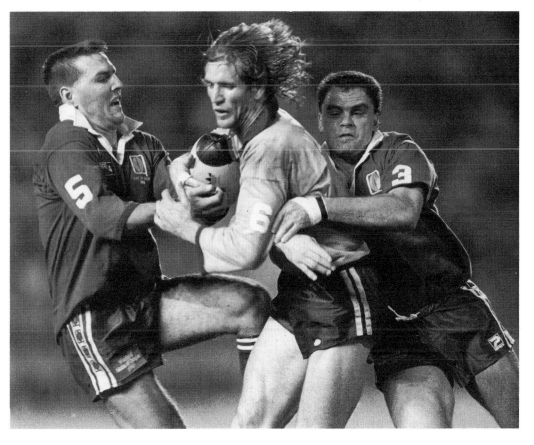

The Test series ended with Australia winning all three matches – 26–6, 8–0, and 22–14 – a result that really did not represent the relative strengths of the two sides.

FOUR

The Season in New Zealand 1989

John Coffey

Auckland again rules the roost among New Zealand provinces, having resisted a formidable challenge from an ambitious Wellington outfit. Although Auckland had not only retained their national first division championship, and had been handsome winners over the Great Britain tourists in 1988, they had suffered one calamitous reversal that year. An inspired Wellington side had emerged 18–10 victors in their second match of the season at Lower Hutt, their first Rugby League success over Auckland since 1913.

It could well have been a unique Wellington double last year. Early in the season Auckland were stunned when Wellington rattled up 18 points in even time at Carlaw Park, but the home team gradually turned the course of the game and, mightily relieved, kept that 75-year unbeaten record intact by 22–18. But there was to be no escape for Auckland in the return fixture as the experienced James Leuluai schemed the upset of the New Zealand representative season.

That was the culmination of many months of preparation by the Wellington coach and former Test hooker, Howie Tamati, who had carefully nurtured the talented youngsters whose achievement had tears welling in the eyes of hardened old internationals up in the grandstand. The result was a crushing blow for the new Auckland coach, Cameron Bell (the father of the Kiwi and Wigan centre, Dean), whose predecessor, Bob Bailey, could boast of a no-loss sequence in five years of domestic football. Even the victory at Great Britain's expense could not have fully salved the wounds inflicted by Wellington.

Both Bell and Tamati started the 1989 southern winter with clear targets. Bell would settle for nothing less than home-and-away wins to lay the ghost that had haunted him over the off-season. Tamati could realistically aim for the first-division championship, and the prospect of Wellington's first-ever triumph at Auckland's Carlaw Park. As it transpired, the other two first-division provinces were soon out of title contention. Canterbury, so recently the team which most troubled Auckland, were beset by transfers and injuries, and the newly-promoted Bay of Plenty side were not competitive.

New Zealand administrators are gradually expanding the provincial competition, and are considering the likes of West Coast and Waikato to boost the numbers. However, for the present, Auckland and Wellington are in a league of their own.

The momentum achieved by Wellington in 1988 was maintained in the first leg of their 1989 confrontation, at Carlaw Park. Auckland were in some trouble when they conceded 6 points. However, Auckland pride was not to be dented on their home patch, and even though injuries reduced their ranks to twelve men in the final quarter the Aucklanders held out for a 12–6 success.

At that stage nothing had changed from the previous year. Auckland had again come from behind to win on Carlaw Park. However, Tamati promised even hotter opposition in the return clash, scheduled for the Basin Reserve, Wellington's cricket Test venue. Wellington expected to have Leuluai back in action, but the still sprightly Kiwi veteran was injured in his first club appearance after returning from Wakefield Trinity.

Worse was to come: the long-serving loose forward, Mike Kuiti (Swinton 1988–89), was a late withdrawal and the captain, Barry Harvey, was switched from hooker to fill the gap. With hindsight, Harvey must regret his decision to play into a strong wind for within a few minutes Bell and his men had their revenge. Kevin Iro, having satisfied himself with a quiet comeback against Canterbury the previous week, ran in two of his 'Wembley specials' and Auckland by half-time were safe at 26–2. In the second half they kept a wind-assisted Wellington at bay for a final scoreline of 32–10. The old order was restored.

No matter how many players Auckland loses to overseas clubs – Shane Cooper was the latest, Kevin Iro and Mark Horo will be next – New Zealand's biggest city has the population and the Rugby League depth to compensate. Bell gave his two hookers, Peter Ropati (Leigh 1988–89) and Duane Mann, equal opportunities in front of the national selectors and they responded eagerly. The prop, Francis Leota, built on his favourable debut season, second-rowers Shane Hansen and Horo complemented each other extremely well, and the Junior Kiwi, Tony Tuimavave, was a busy loose forward.

The goal-kicking scrum-half, Phil Bancroft (a former Rochdale Hornets recruit), stung by Tamati's contention that he was not among the country's top three, was a worthy man-of-the-match.

When injury sidelined the experienced Ron O'Regan (a past Barrow player), burly Kelly Shelford stamped himself as a penetrative stand-off half, and the captain, Paddy Tuimavave (Swinton 1985–86), continued to press for Kiwi recognition at full-back. From an even lot of centres, Mike Patton, overlooked for the first few games, impressed Bell enough to be selected to partner Tony Iro at Wellington.

To the coaches who have painstakingly developed their skills, and the clubs which have fostered their progress, the sight of New Zealand's best young Rugby League players leaving the country to join professional clubs in Australia or Great Britain must be a heartbreaking experience. Though a percentage of those expatriate players have their potential blunted on those professional battlefields, a good number rise to the challenge, thrive in the more competitive atmosphere, and return from time to time as heroes to wear the Kiwi emblem with pride and efficiency.

That New Zealand have been such a threat to Australia, and have slipped ahead of Britain, in Tests over the last decade can be traced largely to the availability of a rich reservoir of overseas-based Kiwis.

Although there were a few signings by Sydney clubs – of Bill Noonan, Bernie Lowther, Henry Tatana and the Sorensen brothers – in the 1970s, it was Hull which opened the floodgates by contracting James Leuluai, Dane

O'Hara and Gary Kemble in 1981. That initiative, and the sour feelings which arose from Cronulla's refusal to release Dane and Kurt Sorensen to assist a struggling Kiwi squad in Australia, led to the International Board ruling that all players must be on stand-by for Tests. In 1983 the Sorensens, Leuluai and Fred Ah Kuoi (then a regular member of the North Sydney reserve team) featured in a stunning victory over Australia at Brisbane, and the Kiwis were flying high again after a decade of disappointments.

The mini-migration has now mushroomed to such an extent that no less than fifty New Zealanders were with British clubs (most of them on temporary off-season transfers) in the 1988–89 northern winter. For the second consecutive year at least one New Zealander was in every trophy-winning first division team: the Iro brothers, Dean Bell, Adrian Shelford and coach Graham Lowe shared Wigan's Challenge Cup, John Player Special Trophy and Lancashire Cup triumphs; Kurt Sorensen, Joe Grima and Emosi Koloto were in the Widnes Championship and Premiership-winning forward packs; and the former All Black Mark Brooke-Cowden helped Leeds clinch the Yorkshire Cup. And they comprise only the tip of this particular Rugby League iceberg. Meanwhile, another twenty or so New Zealanders were playing at various levels of the New South Wales Winfield Cup competition.

It does not take long to come up with a couple of 'Kiwi trial teams' which could meet at a neutral venue – Honolulu? They could be:

Australian-based: Williams (Manly); Elia (Canterbury), Kemp (Newcastle), Sherlock (Easts), Joe Ropati (Manly); Freeman (Balmain), Friend (Norths); Todd (Canberra), Goulding (Newcastle), Dane Sorensen (Cronulla), McGahan (Easts), Stewart (Newcastle), Tuuta (Wests).

British-based: Mercer (Bradford Northern); Shane Horo (Castleford), Bell (Wigan), Kevin Iro (Wigan), Tony Iro (Wigan); Leuluai (Wakefield Trinity), Cooper (St Helens); Grima (Widnes), Peter Ropati (Leigh), Shelford (Wigan), Kurt Sorensen (Widnes), Koloto (Widnes), Mark Horo (Salford).

Only Goulding (a second-rower switched to hooker) has been listed out of a position in which he has played comfortably in international or professional club football. And the 'British' team omits such as Mark Graham, Peter Brown, Dane O'Hara and any number of capable young players hoping to improve themselves away from New Zealand's largely amateur environment.

Transferring players overseas has been a source of valuable income for the code in New Zealand – fees are split between the national administration and the player's former province and club – but has on occasions caused acrimony. Some years ago guidelines were set by which Kiwis would be cleared for a full transfer after playing in six Tests or making two major tours. That proved unfair to some. While those fortunate enough to have toured, say, Britain and France in 1985 and then Australia and Papua New Guinea in 1986 qualified in just a few months without having to play in even one Test, others who had strung together up to five Tests but who had missed one of the 1985 and 1986 tours were left behind lamenting and muttering nasty words about the New Zealand Rugby League.

In 1988 the 'rookie' scheme, by which New Zealand players on the verge of Test or tour selection could be attached to Australian clubs for one season, was introduced. As was feared by the critics, the successful 'rookies' had no wish to return to possible unemployment and meagre match fees; and some of those who languished in lower grades risked losing confidence in their ability. After that first season a former Junior Kiwi centre and full-back, Tony Kemp, successfully argued restraint of trade in the New Zealand High Court and was permitted to sign a long-term contract with the Newcastle Knights.

Kemp's action prompted the New Zealand Rugby League to abandon the old six-Test, two-tour qualifications and treat future transfer applications on their merits. The 'rookie' scheme was roundly criticised by club and provincial coaches and officials and is unlikely to be extended beyond its initial two-year trial period.

On a happier note, much of the vast wealth of Rugby League knowledge accumulated overseas in being passed on to New Zealand youngsters. The former Hull Kingston Rovers and Kiwi team-mates, Mark Broadhurst and Gordon Smith, keep a spring in their steps as rival player-coaches of Papanui and Halswell in the Canterbury provincial competition. While O'Hara continues to display plenty of dash even after 300 appearances for Hull, the other 'originals' are also far from inactive. Leuluai is still a year-round footballer;

Mark Broadhurst, still going forward for his Papanui club in Christchurch in the manner which made him such a respected Kiwi forward and recruit for Hull Kingston Rovers.

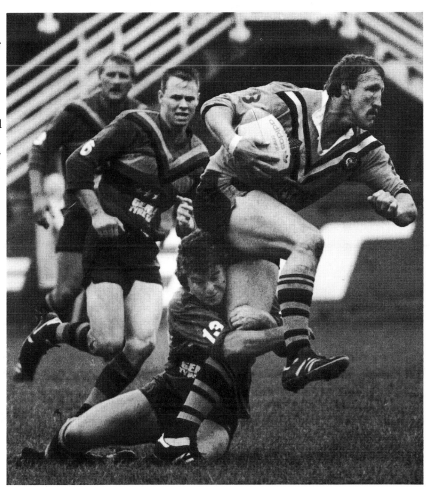

Kemble (and also Ah Kuoi, who was far happier at Hull than he had been at North Sydney) is a club coach in Auckland.

New Zealand does not have the population to support a semi-professional domestic championship, and the upper echelon of officialdom does not subscribe to the widely held opinion that Auckland should lobby for a place in the New South Wales premiership. So the young men will continue to either go west to Sydney or north to Britain and be lost to the local leagues. From time to time they will return, most of them better players, as yet another Kiwi Test coach agonises over the problems of having to mould the styles of three different countries into a winning formula.

Hugh McGahan will realise a cherished ambition when he captains the New Zealand tourists in Great Britain and France from October to December this year. A cruel twist of fate, and a painful twist of McGahan's right knee, prevented him from leading the Kiwis in the 1988 World Cup final. McGahan had already been appointed to the position before it was decided that only a total reconstruction would repair the damaged knee. But as he struggled on crutches when presented with the prestigious Adidas Golden Boot award last year, a fit-again McGahan was always destined to captain his country in a full 1989 international programme.

That Golden Boot award had been made in recognition of McGahan's part in New Zealand's victory over Australia at Brisbane and in leading Eastern Suburbs to third place in the 1987 New South Wales premiership. McGahan admits he enjoys the additional responsibility of calling the tactics for his team-mates. 'You base your game on certain qualities and tend to do certain things in a game,' he says. 'The leadership role just seems to come out in my play, and I don't mind it. It also gives me a chance to yell at a few blokes without them being able to snap back,' he quipped.

McGahan had been a towering figure in directing the Kiwi operations on a remarkable night at Lang Park in 1987. Not only did McGahan and the new Kiwi coach, Tony Gordon, have an inexperienced squad but the captain himself was still suffering from a damaged shoulder.

However McGahan's lingering memory is not of his own performance. 'As far as the actual play went, I was more of a traffic cop telling blokes where to go and what to do. I felt more pride for them – for what they had achieved, for the work they had put in – than for myself,' was his modest summary.

McGahan had previously captained New Zealand during the French section of the 1985 tour, after Mark Graham had been injured in Britain. It was a measure of McGahan's standing among his fellows that there was not even a murmur of dissent when coach Graham Lowe looked beyond his appointed vice-captain, Oslen Filipaina.

Although he was a schoolboy international as a scrum-half, McGahan was always destined for greatness in his preferred loose forward role. He made his Test debut as a replacement in the second Test against Australia at the Sydney Cricket Ground in 1982. Soon afterwards he scored two tries against Papua New Guinea at Port Moresby, but was overlooked for the 1983 home-and-away Tests with Australia.

Miffed at his rejection, McGahan was doubly determined to prove his worth when the Kumuls came to Carlaw Park for a one-off Test later that year. Indeed, he dominated proceedings to such an extent that he established a new world Test record of six tries. Typically, McGahan credits his prop forwards, Kurt Sorensen and Owen Wright, with setting him up for three tries apiece.

The 1989 Kiwis have a proud heritage to uphold. Success in Great Britain is prized by Kiwi teams. It used to be well spaced, too. When Roy Christian's 1971 Kiwis won Tests at Salford and Castleford they were the first to claim a series in Britain since the pioneering 1907–08 All Golds. Now the Kiwis can boast of not having lost a series in Britain since 1965, Mark Graham's 1980 and 1985 teams having shared keenly contested drawn series.

New Zealand face a tough itinerary – three Tests (at Old Trafford, Elland Road and Wigan), a match with Cumbria, and fixtures against the top eight clubs, six of which met the first New Zealanders more than eighty years ago. The past record of the Kiwis' 1989 opponents against them is as follows:

	First met	Won	Lost	Biggest Win	Biggest Defeat
Bradford Northern	1907–08	4	4	38–17 (1926)	15–28 (1965)
Castleford	1947–48	4	1	31–7 (1955)	8–25 (1971)
Featherstone Rovers	1955–56	1	0	7–6 (1955)	No Defeat
Hull	1907–08	7	1	33–10 (1980) 33–10 (1985)	7–13 (1947)
Leeds*	1907–08	8	0	25–5 (1980)	No Defeat
St Helens	1907–08	6	6	46–8 (1985)	7–28 (1965)
Widnes	1907–08	4	3	32–12 (1985)	7–14 (1980) 0–7 (1947)
Wigan	1907–08	4	5	24–10 (1971)	6–28 (1961)

*The 1970 Kiwi World Cup team beat Bradford Northern 28–17 and lost to Leeds 6–11.

NEW ZEALAND v AUSTRALIA TESTS

Christchurch,
9 July
(First Test)

New Zealand 6 Australia 26

Nine months to the day after New Zealand bowed to Australia in the World Cup final at Eden Park the result was repeated at another splendid new Test venue, Queen Elizabeth II Park in Christchurch. The scoreline was again one-sided. Australia had carried off the World Cup by 25–12 in October 1988; the Kiwis were beaten by 6–26 in July in the first match of this three-Test series. There were other similarities. Australia dominated the opening forty minutes each time, leading by 21–0 at half-time in the Cup decider and 20–2 in Christchurch.

After both fixtures there was criticism that New Zealand had been guilty of indulging in over-aggressive defensive tactics in a bid to upset Wally Lewis and his men. But the disappointment after the Test loss was nothing compared to the national despair that had followed the shattering World Cup defeat. Too much was expected of that Kiwi World Cup team. They ran onto Eden Park burdened by the expectations of a whole country and the pressure was too much for them. The aftermath was even worse than the match-day performance. National officials were publicly critical of the efforts of individual players and the sniping carried on through a summer of discontent.

However, that World Cup final will always have a special place in New Zealand Rugby League history. Additional seating was installed to increase the Eden Park capacity to 48,000, thousands of other applications for tickets had to be rejected and there was a massive television audience. Such was the euphoria in New Zealand generally, and especially in Auckland, that the Kiwis even started the match as favourites. However, the Australians were as superb in their preparation as they were to prove on the big day, keeping a low profile and stressing that their players would be well out of season, that Lewis himself was on assignment for a television network at the Olympic Games in Seoul, and that the Kiwis had home ground advantage.

The Australian World Cup side was built round the Sydney Grand Finalists, Canterbury-Bankstown and Balmain. They had thrived on the tensions of the Winfield Cup play-offs, appreciated the rest and were very much in the mood to give Don Furner a perfect coaching farewell. When the Australians returned under Bob Fulton nine months later their Test nucleus was drawn from the highly successful Brisbane Broncos club combination and the triumphant Queensland State of Origin team. Had Allan Langer not been injured, Australia would have had an all-Queensland backline. Similarly, New South Welshmen filled three forward roles at Christchurch largely because of injuries to Gene Miles and Bob Lindner and the surprise omission of Martin Bella.

There was no doubt this time that Australia were hot favourites to confirm the World Cup rankings. The Kiwis looked towards Sydney for their inspiration, but some of the expatriate New Zealanders had very moderate Winfield Cup reputations compared to their Test rivals.

Fulton might not have seen the World Cup final live, or even on video until some months afterwards – he had been lolling on a Honolulu beach when it was played – but he remembered the parts Steve Roach and Paul Sironen filled in the victory. So this time the Australians jogged onto Queen Elizabeth II Park, the 1974 Commonwealth Games stadium, before the biggest Rugby League crowd in Christchurch for more than sixty years, with a massive physical and psychological advantage. Roach, Sironen and Sam Backo all weighed in at well over 100kg. Even Mal Meninga, at centre again after yet another remarkable recovery by his bionic arm, made the Kiwi forwards look like Lilliputians.

The New Zealanders' pre-match plan to run the Australians around did not work out, at least not until the outcome of the Test was no longer in any doubt. There was no lack of courage in the Kiwi display, but the contest was as fair as pitting humans against bulldozers. A rash of handling errors by the Kiwis turned the ball back to their protagonists and the battering down of the New Zealand defences resumed. When Australia played the ball out wide the Kiwis were not always quick enough to prevent breakaways down the flanks. It was not until the second half that the Kiwis looked truly competitive. Perhaps the Australians relaxed in the knowledge of certain victory. But the Kiwis had a more complete pattern on attack after Gary Freeman replaced Clayton Friend at scrum-half.

Paul Sironen, of Australia, gets to grips with the Kiwi captain, Hugh McGahan, in Australia's 26–6 first Test win in Christchurch.

New Zealand: Williams (Manly); Tony Iro (Wigan), Kevin Iro (Wigan), Kemp (Newcastle), Elia (Canterbury-Bankstown); Cooper (St Helens), Friend (North Sydney); Todd (Canberra), Harvey (Wellington), Goulding (Newcastle), McGahan (Eastern Suburbs), Stewart (Newcastle), Tuuta (Western Suburbs)

Substitutes: Freeman (Balmain) for Friend after 40 minutes, Sherlock (Eastern Suburbs), Faimalo (Balmain) and Mark Horo (Auckland) not used

Scorers: try – Elia; goal – Kevin Iro

Australia: Belcher (Canberra); Shearer (Manly), Meninga (Canberra), Currie (Brisbane), Hancock (Brisbane); Lewis (Brisbane), Alexander (Penrith); Backo (Brisbane), Walters (Brisbane), Roach (Balmain), Sironen (Balmain), Clyde (Canberra), Vautin (Manly)

Substitutes: O'Connor (Manly) for Meninga after 75 minutes, McGuire (Balmain) for Roach after 77 minutes, Hasler (Manly) and Trewhella (Eastern Suburbs) not used

Scorers: tries – Currie, Lewis, Walters, Sironen; goals – Meninga (5)

Referee: R. Tennant (Great Britain)

Attendance: 17,000

The Kiwis will still be rebuilding during their 1989 tour of Britain and France. They can, though, recall Adrian Shelford – who did not return early enough from Wigan's American excursion to be considered against Australia – Dean Bell and Kurt Sorensen if they wish. But the actual touring team is more likely to have an Australian, rather than English, professional appearance.

The Kiwi captain, Hugh McGahan, and the full-back, Darrell Williams, made welcome returns in July after missing the World Cup final through injury. Brent Todd and James Goulding, young props who had toured Britain in 1985, were brought back to take on the Australian juggernauts, while the centre, Tony Kemp, and the loose forward, Brendon Tuuta, made Test debuts in Christchurch after making their marks in Sydney on twelve-month 'rookie' clearances. The 'English connection,' once so influential, had been reduced to the Iro brothers, Kevin and Tony, and Shane Cooper.

Understudying these professionals on tour is likely to be a contingent of New Zealand-domiciled players who will serve their apprenticeships on the tour. Among them will be the hooker, Duane Mann, the son of a 1971 Kiwi tourist, Don Mann; Duane replaced Barry Harvey in New Zealand's team for the second Test. Several of the other strong candidates have varying amounts of British experience. Gary Mercer, for example, who has spent the last two northern winters at Bradford Northern and who, despite a disastrous World Cup final as full-back, was selected on the wing for the second Test against Australia in July after Mark Elia had suffered a knee injury, may well be included. Another is the aggressive goal-kicking scrum-half, Phil Bancroft, preferred ahead of Friend as a reserve for the second Test, who spent 1985–86 with Rochdale Hornets.

Among those in the 'shadow' Test line-up, well beaten by Australia in the opening match of the tour but still strong candidates for Britain in October, are the centre David Watson, the stand-off Kelly Shelford, and forwards George Mann and Mike Kuiti, who have all had terms with British clubs. The tour will be the first leg of an intriguing home-and-away series, with Great Britain due to play three Tests in New Zealand in 1990.

Sam Backo, in front, and Steve Roach, the Australian prop forwards who did so much damage to the Kiwis in the first Test of the 1989 series.

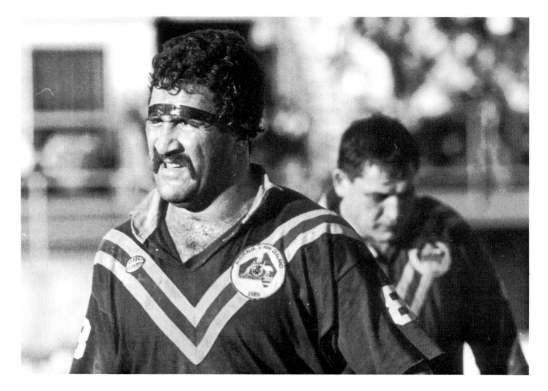

3

Looking Ahead 1989–90

A Preview of the Season and the 1989–90 Fixtures

A Preview of the Season

Mike Rylance

'Small is beautiful', the title of an influential study of economics, became a vogue expression in the 1970s. Its author, Dr E. F. Schumacher, had provided a catchphrase for those who wanted the problems of an increasingly monolithic society to be dealt with on a more human scale. In a sense, Rugby League has had this principle close to its heart for much of its history. Yorkshire and Lancashire people, self-sufficient and independent-minded as they are, perhaps have never quite managed to convince themselves that outsiders were good enough to play their game. In addition, in many of those enclaves where Rugby League has sprung up, its players and administrators have acted in the shadow of a sporting monolith known as Rugby Union. Nowhere is that more true than in France, where *treizistes* often refer to their sport, with a shrug of the shoulders, as being only a minor sport, with none of the satisfactions – the sense of being in control of one's future, for example – that smallness can bring.

In the north of England, however, Rugby League continues to show genuine signs of growth, indicated by increased attendances and the amount of high-level sponsorship it attracts. At the forefront of these sponsors are Dr Schumacher's former employers, British Coal (for whom he acted as economic adviser), who show their faith and interest by backing Rugby League at club, youth and now international level.

Gradually more people outside the north are beginning to realise the sport's attraction and potential, but in terms of its impact on the nation's consciousness it remains unequivocally small. Frustrating as that may be, there is a significant advantage in Rugby League's relatively localized appeal. It should be possible to manage successfully the interests of only five participant countries and to administer without difficulty thirty-odd professional clubs. And yet often the game has seemed to progress in spite of, rather than because of, its administrators, who have been slow to react to the changing needs of those who support it. Like other sports' governing bodies, the Rugby Football League has suffered from the demands of delegates and has not benefited from the management of directors.

The re-structuring of the management of the professional game, just over a year ago, which resulted in the creation of a five-man board of directors and a chief executive, has already shown the effectiveness of a compact and coherent administration. It owes its existence to what David Oxley calls 'the greatest act of unselfishness on the part of any sport's governing body', when council members voted unanimously to hand over the running of the professional game, making the board of directors the envy of other sports in Great Britain.

143

Since its inception, the board has brought about important changes. Appointments made at Chapeltown Road mean that all sections of the game, from players and referees to media and sponsors, are catered for, with an officer of the RFL working in concert with a member of the board. Of the posts created, the two most important, so far as the public is concerned, are the appointment of Fred Lindop as controller of referees and Mike Turner to have charge of merchandising and marketing.

Referees have recently come under more pressure than perhaps ever before. As the speed of the game increases, so it becomes more difficult to control the game effectively. This has been shown by the number of doubtful decisions which have swung the course of matches in the past two seasons. It's a sign of the sportsmanship of Rugby League players and of the effectiveness of the 10-metre rule that some poor decisions are accepted virtually without murmur, but standards of refereeing do need to be raised. Few would envy Fred Lindop his task, but it is a vital one.

Also important is the role of the merchandising and marketing manager. In the past Rugby League has marketed itself badly; in fact is has hardly marketed itself at all. The income to be derived from the merchandise of Rugby League Enterprises is considerable, as is the positive image which the sport can project by means of the quality of its products. Let us hope that the standard of marketing is in keeping with the respect the sport deserves.

By appointments such as these and other decisions it has taken, the board has demonstrated that it can act swiftly, be more open to lobbying and can react more positively to public opinion. Although the full council still ultimately decides whether or not to do this or that, it is the board which identifies the goals to be set.

Ahead lies a more than usually eventful season. The now established Charity Shield match, moved to the mainland from the Isle of Man, took place for the first time in Liverpool at the end of August and in subsequent seasons may be played at Wembley. What was once a jaunt has become designated a big event, an important source of income for its beneficiary, the Rugby League Foundation, which will aid the welfare and development of Rugby League as a whole. In this respect, the decision to take the match to the national stadium may be justified, but some will say that it's unimaginative, that it may dilute the unique appeal of Wembley for Rugby League fans and that there is no guarantee that one set of supporters will want to make a second trip there four months later. Those who would prefer to see the Charity Shield as a movable feast, set up in a different city each year to promote the developing game, will perhaps see the Wembley decision as motivated more by money than by a real concern for development. The Rugby League, however, considers that one-off events serve no real developmental purpose, even though enthusiasts in Newcastle, Bristol or Cardiff would not agree. It certainly makes the International Board's decision (now abandoned) to take the World Club Championship final as a development game to Tokyo, where no Rugby League is played, all the harder to understand.

Instead, the World Club Challenge match will take place at Old Trafford. Widnes, who missed out in 1988, when the idea temporarily foundered, will have their chance to emulate Wigan's 1987 achievement in proving the strength of our domestic scene, when they meet the Sydney champions. It will be a fitting follow-up to the Wigan-Manly clash, which captured the public imagination like no other club match since. This Anglo-Australian challenge is certainly what the fans want to see and it will take place annually unless and until it is replaced by a fully-fledged world club championship. Sadly, the St Estève v. Widnes match at the end of last season showed the ineffectiveness of French competition and organisation, although in the circumstances of Le Pontet's piqued withdrawal, it was courageous of them to go ahead. Unlike the Wigan v. Manly game, it is intended that the Widnes v. Sydney premiers match will be televised nationally. With the right presentation, in front of a mid-week audience, it is a heaven-sent opportunity to show Rugby League at its best, but one can't be confident that the opportunity will be grasped. Nothing arouses Rugby League followers more than the question of television coverage, particularly since the advent of Australian videos has made comparisons possible. It is one area in which the Rugby Football League could be more sensitive to public opinion in taking up the matter of presentation with the television companies.

It would be interesting to see Rugby League follow the practice of cricket and invite a foreign broadcaster accompanying a touring team to commentate on matches, so that an Australian would help to present the World Cup Challenge and a New Zealander would assist with the Kiwi tour matches. It would also help to dispel the notion that Rugby League commentators all come from St Helens.

The Kiwi tour, in the autumn, will be one of their most significant ever. It's a good bet that the tour attendances will show an increase over 1985 and it will be most surprising if the attendance for the first Test at Old Trafford does not exceed that of Headingley in 1985, when an excellent match was watched by only 12,000 spectators.

Despite the memories of that momentous climax to the 1985 tour, at Elland Road, we tend to forget how formidable recent Kiwi teams have been. The 1989 tourists will be keen to maintain their record of not having lost a series in Great Britain since 1965. However, the British will start with a slight edge: they have a stable basic squad of experience and quality. But in the opinion of senior New Zealanders, such as James Leuluai and Kurt Sorensen, the 1989 Kiwis will have some good young players, keen to prove themselves, similar to the tourists of 1980, many of whom, like Gary Kemble, Gary Prohm, Shane Varley, Mark Broadhurst, Mark Graham, Dane O'Hara, Fred Ah Kuoi, Graeme West, Howie and Kevin Tamati and Leuluai himself, went on to become established international figures. In addition to some of their big names who are contracted to English clubs and will be available only for the Tests, New Zealand will have no shortage of talented young individuals eager to pull on the famous black jersey; they cannot be under-estimated.

The third Test in the series, played at Wigan, will again be regarded as a World Cup match, as the next international championship begins its four-year gestation, culminating in a final in 1993. Test matches played by Great Britain in 1990 in New Zealand and Papua New Guinea will be part of the cycle. Although this scheme keeps a Test series alive even if its outcome has already been decided by the second match, and although people will be more familiar

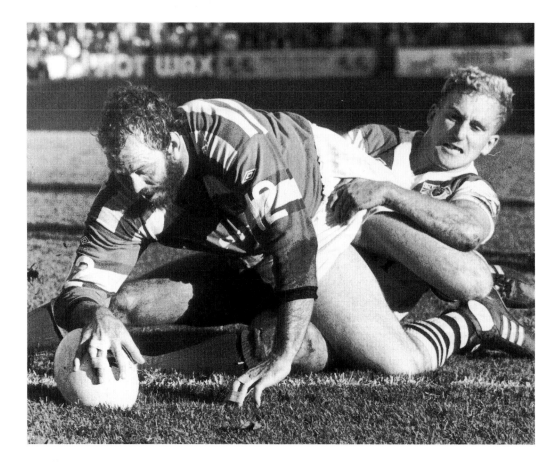

Noel Cleal's distinguished international career is probably now at an end; he was not included in Australia's squad for New Zealand, nor did he take part in the State of Origin series. However, he played for the Rest of the World XIII against Great Britain at Headingley, scoring the Rest's third try, and has now signed for a season with Hull.

with the arrangements this time, four years is a long time to keep public and media interest. Fortunately, in the centenary year of 1995 a more unified competition will take place, with all the impact that that will make, particularly if by then other countries (the RFL has Holland and Germany in mind) have the chance to take part.

The immediate future, even without taking into account the Kiwi tour or the World Club Challenge, has a number of events jostling for our attention. In the early season the Rodstock War of the Roses and the County Cups take place, not forgetting the start of the Stones Bitter Championship, the game's staple competition, which hardly receives the consideration it deserves until clubs come to be relegated or promoted at the end of the season.

The intensity of last year's competition was commented on at length; yet there were few consecutive weeks when the progress of the championship was not interrupted by knock-out competitions. To an outsider it might appear as if the league is only a fill-in between knock-out rounds, or something to do for those clubs (the majority, in fact) whose interest in a given cup competition is soon terminated. In England the value of the league championship – the most enduring test of a team – is not sufficiently emphasized. By contrast the County

Cups and the former John Player Trophy, now re-named the Regal Trophy, do not create the same sense of anticipation among supporters, particularly since giant-killers are in short supply. Though the revenue from sponsorship is important, it is also important to establish priorities, as league matches continue to attract bigger crowds. At the moment the profusion of different competitions makes the season's programme a clutter: people new to the game are confused by it and the conflict of interest experienced by some clubs as they try to maintain an interest in both cup and league leads to some embarrassing performances.

Many disinterested observers would also say that three clubs relegated out of fourteen is too many, because of the constant struggle of about half the first-division teams to avoid the drop. On the other hand, twenty-one second-division clubs are interested in being promoted, or so they claim, so that the system will remain as it is for the immediate future. But perhaps not beyond that. 'There's no question about it: we are committed to a three-division structure,' says David Oxley, 'when the numbers are right. The minimum would be thirty-six teams.' The shortfall of one, which produces an odd number of teams in the second division, will do nothing to solve the problem of the fixture formula, though whichever opponents they play, each club will at least play them home and away.

Last season it was said that the first division was the most competitive for years. This year there will be more than the usual amount of attention focused on the second division. Halifax, Hull KR and Oldham will certainly increase the attendances and there is a strong possibility that one of them, probably Halifax, will become the best-supported second-division club ever. It would be a brave man who would bet against those three clubs going straight back to the first division. Halifax, with John Dorahy in control, a most knowledgeable and likeable man, in the Anderson-Eadie line, will be too strong for most teams, as will Hull KR, who make a fresh start away from the unmourned Craven Park. Although Oldham have had their problems off the field, they have shown a concern for the longer term by investing in promising junior talent, and deserve to succeed. There will be some much-needed attention directed towards Fulham, who welcome the controversial Ross Strudwick. It could turn out to be a turning point both for coach and club. In any event, Strudwick and the newly-appointed development officer should ensure a bigger Rugby League presence in the capital than for some years.

One wishes that the Chorley-Trafford resolution could arouse a similar amount of positive interest. Thanks to a newly-formed club under the aegis of Chorley AFC, professional Rugby League will continue to be played in the county of Lancashire. What was Chorley Borough, and Blackpool and Springfield before that, becomes Trafford and will play at Altrincham. It may be their last chance to establish themselves, though local council support will improve their chances of success. There may be a last chance, too, for Mansfield, who, after Alfreton and Sutton, go for the other extreme in Nottingham. This is a venture which needs to succeed, if only because of the high profile which a big-city name gives to the sport in general. One can't help thinking that it's unfortunate that there is no mechanism in Rugby League, as there is in soccer, by which non-league clubs can be admitted to professional status; clubs which

Andy Currier of Widnes was one of the British Rugby League players who spent the northern summer in Australia. Currier had a successful season with Balmain.

are already established on a sound footing, with roots in the area, with people in control who have experience, albeit at a different level, of running a Rugby League club. Maybe in the course of time the National Amateur League will become that bridge.

Also on the move, from a stadium which belonged to another era, are York. Their suburban site at Monks Cross may or may not be an example for other clubs to follow. Much will depend on the extent to which local councils will be prepared to allow the land, but the dilapidated state of some grounds, among them some of the oldest in the League, requires drastic action. York will be well in advance of the minimum standards charter which the RFL is going to enforce in order to ensure a certain degree of comfort and safety for the modern-day spectator. Quite rightly the RFL recognizes that, although crowds are increasing, they will have to be provided for if they are to be kept.

Both York and Hull KR have reacted to the effects of the Bradford City fire disaster, which cost the game some £5 million to bring its stadiums to licensable standards. The Hillsborough disaster makes one wonder whether further measures will need to be taken. It is thought that, although there will undoubtedly be lessons to be learned from the inquiry's report, especially in terms of organization of crowds, the consequences will not be as far-reaching as after Bradford. Nor are there plans by the government to impose identity cards on Rugby League. However the RFL recognizes that hooliganism within the sport, though minor, is not a matter to shrink away from: it will pursue its policy to 'locate, eject, arrest and prosecute' all trouble-makers at its matches. It is a problem which the RFL treats very seriously. Its chairman's club, Featherstone Rovers, is one which is presently more affected than some.

The first division shows every sign of being as fascinating as it was last season. Of the three promoted clubs trying to emulate Featherstone's and Wakefield's feat of breaking the yo-yo syndrome, Leigh and Barrow have been running an almost continuous shuttle for some years now. At the end of last season Leigh looked to have the best chance of survival of the three, but the same might have been said of Oldham the season before. Barrow's return to the top flight is important for Rugby League in the north-west and it is pleasing to see a reward for Rod Reddy's efforts with his young team. Sheffield's entry into the big league for the first time in their brief history will be the most interesting. Managed in a way which could profitably be copied by other clubs, both old and new, the Eagles have succeeded without gaining the support of the Sheffield public in any number. If only because of away teams' support, their attendances will improve, but it may be that the local publicity surrounding their promotion will be translated into increased home support. They, like the other two promoted clubs, will have had to strengthen the team, but Gary Hetherington's ability to give both local and foreign players ideals other than mere money could be a key factor. It will be a major triumph if Sheffield survive in the first division.

At the top, it will be interesting to see who can deny Widnes a record third consecutive championship. Their abundance of all-round talent can only be matched by Leeds and Wigan, whose ability to buy in top-class talent cannot be taken lightly and, apart from any other factor, makes them a force to be reckoned with. In the case of Leeds, much will be hoped of and expected from

Peter Sterling, a truly model player, although he will find British conditions rather different from when he played his last outstanding season here with Hull in 1984–85. Wigan will be looking for continuity which may prove elusive. No one can be envied the task of following Graham Lowe's achievements and the relationship he built up with the players over three years. The fact that five Wigan players who played during the summer in Australia made themselves available for the Milwaukee match shows not only their commitment to the project but also their loyalty to their coach. Wigan will be hoping that they do not suffer as a consequence of having key players playing too strenuous a programme, since all five, except Steve Hampson, have played continuously for two years and all will be involved in representative matches when they return. They will also have to come back to a new regime.

There will be other first-division clubs which find themselves at a cross-roads: Warrington, for example, who just avoided relegation and whose attendances last year showed a percentage decrease, unlike any other first-division club; and neighbours St Helens. Like many other clubs, St Helens's chances of success will depend on close-season acquisitions. Their reaction to the Cup final defeat by transfer-listing half the team seemed to owe more to emotion than reason. After each of three recent Wembley defeats, Alex Murphy has particularly criticised the failings of his overseas players: O'Connor and Vautin thus succeeded Mark Elia (1987) and Howie Tamati (1984). He has vowed no more short-term contracts for overseas players. For the sake of credibility he must hope that his third expensive signing from Welsh Rugby Union, Jonathan Griffiths, succeeds where Stuart Evans and Mike Carrington have failed to impress, although the idea of building a team around a comparatively inexperienced Welsh scrum-half has a familiar if unsuccessful ring to it.

Hull's heartening recovery of last season can be built upon: the sudden blossoming of players who had until last season shown only promise is a tribute to Brian Smith's coaching and player-management. Always prepared to question procedures hallowed by time but not much else, Smith brought a freshness of approach to Humberside when it was most needed. His appointment at Hull was yet another example of how master coach Jack Gibson's prophecy of some five years ago has been fulfilled. At the time when English clubs were scrambling after Australian players, who had just been made available following the lifting of the international transfers ban, Gibson advised that it would make much more sense to import coaches rather than players because of their long-term benefit and because their effect on a club would be more radical. Smith is one of half a dozen overseas coaches who have made a deep impression on their club and have proved correct a prediction that must, to many people, have seemed improbable at the time.

Hull's signing of the 1986 Kangaroo, Steve Folkes, on a two-year contract is a typically thoughtful one and is based not only on his ability as a player but also on his positive attitude, particularly to the younger players around him – which, of course, is how it should be. There has been plenty of criticism, over the past couple of seasons, of imported Australian players for failing to meet expectations, however unrealistic those hopes may have been. Australian players, as they themselves often tell us, are only human – but they become even more human when they discover that you don't have to do that much to fulfil an English short-term contract, especially if the coaching and disciplinary set-up is more lax than back home.

A short-term contract can have a value, and certainly Australian clubs still think it worthwhile to import top English players on that basis, but it cannot be a substitute for team-building. Unfortunately some coaches and directors find it hard to see beyond the short-term. But short-term it will be this season, at least for first-grade Sydney players, who will have to return by early February, ready for the lucrative Panasonic Cup competition. Negotiations will hopefully ensure that Australian players with clubs still involved in the Challenge Cup will be allowed to stay up to and including the third round, with the mandatory return for the semi-final and final, in order to avoid the kind of wrangling which took place between St Helens and Manly last year. Longer contracts, perhaps offered to players who no longer see their future in Sydney, will begin to look more attractive. The more resourceful clubs will also continue to show an interest in young Australians and New Zealanders waiting for the chance to make their mark, and who need not cost huge amounts of money.

Some of the problems of player recruitment stem from the fact that professional clubs tend to expect some other source to provide players for them: the amateur game, Australia or New Zealand, Rugby Union, or other professional clubs. They consider that their money, whether they actually have it to spend or not, is enough. To encourage clubs to spend within their means, the RFL will in future demand that half the transfer fee is paid immediately and the rest within twelve months. But too many professional clubs still do not see themselves as part of the system which produces Rugby League players. Sheffield Eagles is a rare example of a club which is prepared to invest time, effort and money in the amateur and schoolboy game and which sees no artificial division between amateur and professional Rugby League.

The emergence last season of the mid-week youth leagues should have seen professionals and amateurs working side by side in most areas. In this way the most talented young players would come together weekly to benefit from the facilities and expertise which a professional club can offer, and play matches every three weeks. Although seventy-five per cent of matches in this British Coal-sponsored league were played, in some areas there was little co-operation between the professional club and the amateurs within the district association. Although in some places like St Helens the scheme worked well, in others it hardly got going: Leeds, for example, where the professional club took no interest, was represented by a single amateur club; and Bradford had no representation at all.

The RFL admits that the scheme stands or falls by the input the professional clubs make. It is unfortunate that at the end of last season some professional clubs tried to undermine the scheme by re-forming their own Colts teams, in the guise of an Under-20s league, under their direct control. BARLA, of course, has its part to play as well in order to make the scheme work, by properly organising the regular weekend youth football from which the mid-week youth leagues will take their players. Since there is a three-year commitment to the scheme, closer control over individual district associations by both the RFL and BARLA will hopefully bring about an improvement in this most important development area.

151

Ellery Hanley enjoyed an extremely successful British summer season with Wests and, with Garry Schofield, helped them to make a real mark on the Sydney League.

The Rugby League adminstration has also shown the foresight to provide for international development. The International Board's provision of two per cent of international match receipts towards development is an encouraging step. There are various areas where the money could be used. Perhaps Holland or Germany, where a 'big initiative', in David Oxley's words, is taking place, will be considered. France should remain a priority area for assistance, on the grounds that you must hang on to what you've got. In the face of Rugby Union domination and sometimes their own inadequacies they need all the help they can get. It is certainly sad to see a major Rugby League-playing country, where the game was once so vibrant, enduring its present turmoil. But France will at least fulfil all its fixtures in the next World Cup series, making a mini-tour of Australia and possibly Papua New Guinea.

One area which is not earmarked for further financial assistance is the USA. Despite the success of the Wigan–Warrington match in attracting a very satisfactory crowd of 18,000 and creating a good deal of interest in the Milwaukee region; despite all the groundwork done over more than twelve years by Mike Mayer, when so many times the cause seemd lost, he has not managed to win the confidence of the International Board. Since no one else seems capable of doing what he has achieved, it looks as if the Board is not interested in taking the game across the Atlantic. As almost everyone appreciates, the potential for expansion into the world's largest sporting and television market is enormous. A relatively slight impact by American standards would have a substantial effect on our own narrow-based game.

Why try to expand abroad, some might say, when the sport is still very limited geographically in Britain? But international competition brings a variety of benefits and interests to our domestic competition, the strength of which is partly gauged by the success of the national team. International sport, like international anything else, broadens horizons. Those of us fortunate to have seen an American broadcast of the 1984 Challenge Cup final have appreciated the professionalism of the American approach and the sense of anticipation they managed to create. And you only need to think back seven years to see how one country's standards, particularly on the field of play, have influenced another's.

But there are of course serious attempts at development going on in Britain. The Rugby League Foundation has been responsible for development officers in key areas and will soon have a complement of nearly twenty. This progress stands comparison with that of almost any other sport. It's not simply in trying to add to the numbers of people and clubs playing Rugby League that the development officer's job consists, but also in acting as a support system for the often fragile structures set up by enthusiasts, often in untraditional areas. The appointment of two men to cover Student Rugby League has been a long time coming but is certain to bring results. They will ensure Rugby League's presence in this vital but volatile sector, which will, in the course of time, feed back into the game. The main, eventual involvement of students, or rather former students, will be in terms of administration and we can see by the way in which some clubs are run that there is room for intelligent support here.

The 1989–90 season will very likely show the continuing success of Rugby League as an entertainment sport, but that success will be more or less confined to the upper echelons of the game. Unfortunately the majority of professional clubs may simply stagnate. True, they can't all be winners, but there need not be so many in a desperate financial state, living a hand-to-mouth existence, putting on matches at equally desperate-looking grounds. As more money comes into Rugby League, more money polarises around the big clubs, who offer big contracts and big transfer fees which others cannot match. Fortunately there is, at the moment, still a chance for the smaller club, like Featherstone Rovers, to compete, but for how much longer?

Sensibly-run clubs have always recognised the need to become involved in the development of junior talent. The professional club becomes the apex of a system which begins at schoolboy level, so that it should become the ambition of a young player to play for his local club, which in turn takes an interest in the amateur game in the area.

But that is an ideal situation. In many areas Rugby League is hopelessly fragmented: there might be Rugby League played in the middle school, but not at the secondary; there might be a local amateur team, but only for open-age; a player might have taken the game up at university, but then reverts to Rugby Union in the place he chooses to live in, because there is no amateur Rugby League club. There is a need for a unified aim.

At the beginning of a new season, one which offers the possibility of real progress, it is worth bearing in mind another observation by Dr Schumacher: 'When it comes to action, we obviously need small units. But when it comes to the world of ideas, principles or ethics . . . we need to recognise unity . . . and base our actions on this recognition.'

The Rugby Football League
Principal Dates, 1989–90

1989	August 27	CIS Insurance Charity Shield: Widnes v. Wigan (at Anfield, Liverpool)
	September 3	Stones Bitter Championship season begins
	September 17	County Cup competitions (1st round)
	September 20	Rodstock War of the Roses: Yorkshire v. Lancashire County of Origin (at Central Park, Wigan)
	September 27	County Cup competitions (2nd round)
	October 4	Foster's World Club Challenge: Widnes v. Australian Grand Final Winner (at Old Trafford, Manchester)
	October 5	Grünhalle Lager Lancashire Cup semi-finals
	October 11	John Smith's Yorkshire Cup semi-finals
	October 15	Grünhalle Lager Lancashire Cup final
	October 21	British Coal Test: Great Britain v. New Zealand (1) (at Old Trafford, Manchester)
	October 28	British Coal Test: Great Britain v. New Zealand (2) (at Elland Road, Leeds)
	November 5	John Smith's Yorkshire Cup final
	November 11	British Coal Test: Great Britain v. New Zealand (3) (at Central Park, Wigan)
	December 2	Regal Trophy (1st round)
	December 9	Regal Trophy (2nd round)
	December 16	Regal Trophy (3rd round)
	December 23	Regal Trophy (semi-final 1)
	December 30	Regal Trophy (semi-final 2)
1990	January 13	Regal Trophy final
	January 21	British Coal Under-21 International: France v. Great Britain (at Villeneuve)
	January 27	Silk Cut Challenge Cup (1st round)
	February 10	Silk Cut Challenge Cup (2nd round)
	February 16	British Coal Under-21 International: Great Britain v. France (venue to be decided)
	February 24	Silk Cut Challenge Cup (3rd round)
	March 10	Silk Cut Challenge Cup (semi-final 1)
	March 18	British Coal Test: France v. Great Britain (at Carcassonne)
	March 31	Silk Cut Challenge Cup (semi-final 2)
	April 7	British Coal Test: Great Britain v. France (venue to be decided)
	April 28	Silk Cut Challenge Cup final (at Wembley Stadium)
	May 13	Stones Bitter Premiership finals (at Old Trafford, Manchester)

The Rugby Football League
The New Zealand Tour, 1989

Sunday
October 1   v.   St Helens

Tuesday
October 3   v.   Castleford

Sunday
October 8   v.   Wigan

Wednesday
October 11   v.   Bradford Northern

Sunday
October 15   v.   Leeds

Tuesday
October 17   v.   Cumbria (at Whitehaven)

Saturday
October 21   v.   Great Britain (1)
                  (at Old Trafford, Manchester)

Saturday
October 28   v.   Great Britain (2)
                  (at Elland Road, Leeds)

Wednesday
November 1   v.   Featherstone Rovers

Sunday
November 5   v.   Widnes

Tuesday
November 7   v.   Hull

Saturday
November 11   v.   Great Britain (3)
                   (at Central Park, Wigan)

The Rugby Football League
Stones Bitter Championship, 1989–1990

First Division Fixtures

1989	Bradford N.	v.	Hull
Sunday	Castleford	v.	Featherstone R.
September 3	Leeds	v.	Wakefield T.
	Leigh	v.	Barrow
	Sheffield E.	v.	St Helens
	Widnes	v.	Salford
	Wigan	v.	Warrington

| Wednesday | Leigh | v. | Wigan |
| September 6 | | | |

Sunday	Barrow	v.	Leeds
September 10	Featherstone R.	v.	Sheffield E.
	Hull	v.	Widnes
	St Helens	v.	Castleford
	Salford	v.	Wigan
	Wakefield T.	v.	Leigh
	Warrington	v.	Bradford N.

Sunday	Bradford N.	v.	St Helens
September 24	Castleford	v.	Hull
	Leeds	v.	Salford
	Leigh	v.	Warrington
	Sheffield E.	v.	Barrow
	Widnes	v.	Featherstone R.
	Wigan	v.	Wakefield T.

Sunday	Barrow	v.	Wigan
October 1	Featherstone R.	v.	Leigh
	Hull	v.	Leeds
	Salford	v.	Bradford N.
	Wakefield T.	v.	Sheffield E.
	Warrington	v.	Castleford
	St Helens	v.	New Zealand

| Tuesday | Castleford | v. | New Zealand |
| October 3 | | | |

Sunday	Bradford N.	v.	Barrow
October 8	Featherstone R.	v.	Leeds
	Salford	v.	Leigh
	Sheffield E.	v.	Widnes
	Wakefield T.	v.	St Helens
	Warrington	v.	Hull
	Wigan	v.	New Zealand

| Wednesday | Bradford N. | v. | New Zealand |
| October 11 | | | |

Sunday	Barrow	v.	Warrington
October 15	Castleford	v.	Sheffield E.
	Hull	v.	Salford
	St Helens	v.	Featherstone R.
	Widnes	v.	Wakefield T.
	Leeds	v.	New Zealand

| Tuesday | Cumbria | v. | New Zealand |
| October 17 | | | |

Sunday	Bradford N.	v.	Leigh
October 29	Featherstone R.	v.	Barrow
	Salford	v.	Widnes
	Sheffield E.	v.	Leeds
	Wakefield T.	v.	Hull
	Warrington	v.	St Helens
	Wigan	v.	Castleford

| Wednesday | Featherstone R. | v. | New Zealand |
| November 1 | | | |

Sunday	Barrow	v.	Wakefield T.
November 5	Castleford	v.	Bradford N.
	Leeds	v.	Warrington
	Leigh	v.	Featherstone R.
	St Helens	v.	Salford
	Sheffield E.	v.	Wigan
	Widnes	v.	New Zealand

| Tuesday | Hull | v. | New Zealand |
| November 7 | | | |

Sunday	Bradford N.	v.	Wigan
November 12	Featherstone R.	v.	Hull
	St Helens	v.	Barrow
	Salford	v.	Leeds
	Wakefield T.	v.	Castleford
	Warrington	v.	Sheffield E.
	Widnes	v.	Leigh

Sunday	Barrow	v.	Salford
November 19	Castleford	v.	Warrington
	Hull	v.	St Helens
	Leeds	v.	Widnes
	Leigh	v.	Wakefield T.
	Sheffield E.	v.	Bradford N.
	Wigan	v.	Featherstone R.

Sunday November 26	Bradford N.	v.	Leeds
	Featherstone R.	v.	St Helens
	Salford	v.	Sheffield E.
	Wakefield T.	v.	Barrow
	Warrington	v.	Leigh
	Widnes	v.	Castleford
	Wigan	v.	Hull
Sunday December 17	Barrow	v.	Widnes
	Castleford	v.	Wigan
	Hull	v.	Leigh
	St Helens	v.	Bradford N.
	Sheffield E.	v.	Featherstone R.
	Warrington	v.	Salford
Tuesday December 26 Boxing Day	Featherstone R.	v.	Wakefield T.
	Hull	v.	Sheffield E.
	Leeds	v.	Castleford
	Leigh	v.	Salford
	Widnes	v.	Warrington
	Wigan	v.	St Helens
Sunday December 31	Barrow	v.	Sheffield E.
1990 Monday January 1 New Year's Day	Bradford N.	v.	Castleford
	Leeds	v.	Hull
	St Helens	v.	Widnes
	Wakefield T.	v.	Featherstone R.
	Warrington	v.	Wigan
Sunday January 7	Castleford	v.	Wakefield T.
	Hull	v.	Barrow
	Leigh	v.	St Helens
	Salford	v.	Featherstone R.
	Sheffield E.	v.	Warrington
	Widnes	v.	Leeds
	Wigan	v.	Bradford N.
Sunday January 14	Bradford N.	v.	Widnes
	Featherstone R.	v.	Castleford
	Leeds	v.	Leigh
	St Helens	v.	Hull
	Wakefield T.	v.	Salford
	Warrington	v.	Barrow
	Wigan	v.	Sheffield E.
Sunday January 21	Barrow	v.	Featherstone R.
	Castleford	v.	Widnes
	Hull	v.	Wigan
	Leeds	v.	Bradford N.
	Leigh	v.	Sheffield E.
	Salford	v.	St Helens
	Wakefield T.	v.	Warrington
Sunday February 4	Featherstone R.	v.	Warrington
	Hull	v.	Castleford
	Leigh	v.	Bradford N.
	Salford	v.	Barrow
	Sheffield E.	v.	Wakefield T.
	St Helens	v.	Leeds
	Widnes	v.	Wigan

Sunday February 18	Barrow	v.	St Helens
	Bradford N.	v.	Featherstone R.
	Castleford	v.	Leigh
	Leeds	v.	Sheffield E.
	Warrington	v.	Wakefield T.
	Widnes	v.	Hull
	Wigan	v.	Salford
Sunday February 25	Featherstone R.	v.	Widnes
	Hull	v.	Bradford N.
	Leigh	v.	Leeds
	St Helens	v.	Warrington
	Salford	v.	Castleford
	Wigan	v.	Barrow
Sunday March 4	Barrow	v.	Hull
	Bradford N.	v.	Salford
	Castleford	v.	St Helens
	Leeds	v.	Wigan
	Sheffield E.	v.	Leigh
	Wakefield T.	v.	Widnes
	Warrington	v.	Featherstone R.
Sunday March 11	Barrow	v.	Leigh
	Featherstone R.	v.	Salford
	Hull	v.	Wakefield T.
	Sheffield E.	v.	Castleford
	Warrington	v.	Leeds
	Widnes	v.	Bradford N.
Sunday March 18	Bradford N.	v.	Sheffield E.
	Featherstone R.	v.	Wigan
	Leeds	v.	Barrow
	Leigh	v.	Widnes
	St Helens	v.	Wakefield T.
	Salford	v.	Hull
Sunday March 25	Bradford N.	v.	Warrington
	Castleford	v.	Barrow
	Hull	v.	Featherstone R.
	St Helens	v.	Leigh
	Sheffield E.	v.	Salford
	Wakefield T.	v.	Leeds
	Wigan	v.	Widnes
Sunday April 1	Barrow	v.	Bradford N.
	Castleford	v.	Salford
	Leeds	v.	St Helens
	Leigh	v.	Hull
	Wakefield T.	v.	Wigan
	Widnes	v.	Sheffield E.
Sunday April 8	Featherstone R.	v.	Bradford N.
	Hull	v.	Warrington
	Leigh	v.	Castleford
	St Helens	v.	Sheffield E.
	Salford	v.	Wakefield T.
	Widnes	v.	Barrow
	Wigan	v.	Leeds

Good Friday April 13	Barrow	v.	Castleford		Easter Monday April 16	Castleford	v.	Leeds
	Bradford N.	v.	Wakefield T.			Salford	v.	Warrington
	Leeds	v.	Featherstone R.			Wakefield T.	v.	Bradford N.
	St Helens	v.	Wigan			Widnes	v.	St Helens
	Warrington	v.	Widnes			Wigan	v.	Leigh
Sunday April 15	Sheffield E.	v.	Hull					

Second Division Fixtures

1989
Sunday
September 3

Batley	v.	Nottingham City
Carlisle	v.	Runcorn H.
Doncaster	v.	Dewsbury
Fulham	v.	Ryedale York
Halifax	v.	Rochdale H.
Hunslet	v.	Bramley
Keighley	v.	Hull KR.
Oldham	v.	Workington T.
Swinton	v.	Chorley
Whitehaven	v.	Huddersfield

Wednesday
September 6

Carlisle	v.	Keighley
Chorley	v.	Bramley
Hunslet	v.	Ryedale York
Runcorn H.	v.	Batley
Trafford B.	v.	Swinton
Whitehaven	v.	Rochdale H.

Sunday
September 10

Batley	v.	Ryedale York
Bramley	v.	Doncaster
Chorley	v.	Whitehaven
Dewsbury	v.	Keighley
Halifax	v.	Oldham
Huddersfield	v.	Fulham
Nottingham City	v.	Hunslet
Rochdale H.	v.	Swinton
Trafford B.	v.	Runcorn H.
Workington T.	v.	Carlisle

Wednesday
September 13

Huddersfield	v.	Hunslet
Keighley	v.	Whitehaven

Sunday
September 24

Batley	v.	Bramley
Chorley	v.	Fulham
Doncaster	v.	Runcorn H.
Huddersfield	v.	Workington T.
Hull KR.	v.	Trafford B.
Keighley	v.	Nottingham City
Rochdale H.	v.	Dewsbury
Swinton	v.	Ryedale York
Whitehaven	v.	Hunslet

Sunday
October 1

Bramley	v.	Rochdale H.
Chorley	v.	Keighley
Dewsbury	v.	Swinton
Doncaster	v.	Whitehaven
Fulham	v.	Carlisle
Hunslet	v.	Batley
Nottingham City	v.	Halifax
Oldham	v.	Hull KR.
Runcorn H.	v.	Huddersfield
Workington T.	v.	Ryedale York

Sunday
October 8

Batley	v.	Swinton
Bramley	v.	Chorley
Carlisle	v.	Workington T.
Halifax	v.	Doncaster
Huddersfield	v.	Trafford B.
Hull KR.	v.	Nottingham City
Hunslet	v.	Dewsbury
Runcorn H.	v.	Oldham
Ryedale York	v.	Keighley
Whitehaven	v.	Fulham

Sunday
October 15

Chorley	v.	Hunslet
Dewsbury	v.	Runcorn H.
Doncaster	v.	Ryedale York
Fulham	v.	Rochdale H.
Huddersfield	v.	Whitehaven
Nottingham City	v.	Batley
Oldham	v.	Halifax
Swinton	v.	Carlisle
Trafford B.	v.	Keighley
Workington T.	v.	Bramley

Sunday
October 22

Batley	v.	Whitehaven
Carlisle	v.	Oldham
Fulham	v.	Bramley
Halifax	v.	Dewsbury
Hull KR.	v.	Swinton
Keighley	v.	Doncaster
Rochdale H.	v.	Workington T.
Runcorn H.	v.	Nottingham City
Trafford B.	v.	Hunslet

The 1989-90 Fixtures

Sunday October 29	Bramley	v.	Halifax
	Dewsbury	v.	Chorley
	Doncaster	v.	Workington T.
	Hull KR.	v.	Fulham
	Hunslet	v.	Carlisle
	Keighley	v.	Trafford B.
	Nottingham City	v.	Rochdale H.
	Oldham	v.	Batley
	Ryedale York	v.	Huddersfield
	Whitehaven	v.	Swinton
Sunday November 5	Chorley	v.	Nottingham City
	Dewsbury	v.	Carlisle
	Doncaster	v.	Oldham
	Fulham	v.	Whitehaven
	Halifax	v.	Hull KR.
	Keighley	v.	Batley
	Rochdale H.	v.	Runcorn H.
	Ryedale York	v.	Hunslet
	Swinton	v.	Bramley
	Workington T.	v.	Trafford B.
Sunday November 12	Batley	v.	Runcorn H.
	Bramley	v.	Fulham
	Carlisle	v.	Ryedale York
	Chorley	v.	Dewsbury
	Hull KR.	v.	Workington T.
	Hunslet	v.	Huddersfield
	Nottingham City	v.	Swinton
	Oldham	v.	Keighley
	Trafford B.	v.	Halifax
	Whitehaven	v.	Doncaster
Sunday November 19	Dewsbury	v.	Hunslet
	Doncaster	v.	Trafford B.
	Fulham	v.	Oldham
	Halifax	v.	Chorley
	Huddersfield	v.	Nottingham City
	Keighley	v.	Carlisle
	Rochdale H.	v.	Ryedale York
	Runcorn H.	v.	Bramley
	Swinton	v.	Hull KR.
	Workington T.	v.	Batley
Sunday November 26	Batley	v.	Fulham
	Bramley	v.	Huddersfield
	Carlisle	v.	Halifax
	Hull KR.	v.	Dewsbury
	Hunslet	v.	Rochdale H.
	Nottingham City	v.	Runcorn H.
	Oldham	v.	Doncaster
	Ryedale York	v.	Chorley
	Trafford B.	v.	Workington T.
	Whitehaven	v.	Keighley
Sunday December 17	Batley	v.	Trafford B.
	Carlisle	v.	Nottingham City
	Chorley	v.	Swinton
	Dewsbury	v.	Halifax
	Doncaster	v.	Hunslet
	Fulham	v.	Hull KR.
	Huddersfield	v.	Ryedale York
	Rochdale H.	v.	Bramley
	Runcorn H.	v.	Whitehaven
	Workington T.	v.	Oldham

Tuesday December 26 Boxing Day	Batley	v.	Dewsbury
	Bramley	v.	Keighley
	Halifax	v.	Huddersfield
	Hull KR.	v.	Ryedale York
	Hunslet	v.	Chorley
	Nottingham City	v.	Doncaster
	Rochdale H.	v.	Oldham
	Runcorn H.	v.	Carlisle
	Swinton	v.	Trafford B.
	Workington T.	v.	Whitehaven
Thursday December 28	Trafford B.	v.	Carlisle
Sunday December 31	Dewsbury	v.	Batley
	Doncaster	v.	Fulham
	Huddersfield	v.	Keighley
	Hunslet	v.	Hull KR
	Rydale York	v.	Workington T.
1990 Monday January 1 New Year's Day	Chorley	v.	Runcorn H.
	Halifax	v.	Bramley
	Oldham	v.	Swinton
	Trafford B.	v.	Rochdale H.
	Whitehaven	v.	Carlisle
Sunday January 7	Bramley	v.	Batley
	Carlisle	v.	Swinton
	Dewsbury	v.	Doncaster
	Fulham	v.	Trafford B.
	Huddersfield	v.	Runcorn H.
	Keighley	v.	Rochdale H.
	Nottingham City	v.	Hull KR.
	Oldham	v.	Hunslet
	Rydale York	v.	Halifax
	Workington T.	v.	Chorley
Sunday January 14	Batley	v.	Keighley
	Bramley	v.	Workington T.
	Hull KR.	v.	Oldham
	Hunslet	v.	Nottingham City
	Rochdale H.	v.	Fulham
	Runcorn H.	v.	Dewsbury
	Ryedale York	v.	Carlisle
	Swinton	v.	Huddersfield
	Trafford B.	v.	Chorley
	Whitehaven	v.	Halifax
Sunday January 21	Carlisle	v.	Bramley
	Chorley	v.	Oldham
	Doncaster	v.	Keighley
	Fulham	v.	Batley
	Rochdale H.	v.	Whitehaven
	Runcorn H.	v.	Ryedale York
	Swinton	v.	Nottingham City
	Trafford B.	v.	Huddersfield
	Workington T.	v.	Hull KR.

The 1989–90 Fixtures

Sunday February 4		
Bramley	v.	Hull KR.
Chorley	v.	Workington T.
Hunslet	v.	Doncaster
Keighley	v.	Dewsbury
Nottingham City	v.	Huddersfield
Oldham	v.	Fulham
Ryedale York	v.	Rochdale H.
Trafford B.	v.	Batley
Whitehaven	v.	Runcorn H.

Sunday February 18		
Dewsbury	v.	Rochdale H.
Doncaster	v.	Bramley
Halifax	v.	Rydale York
Hull KR.	v.	Runcorn H.
Nottingham City	v.	Fulham
Oldham	v.	Chorley
Swinton	v.	Whitehaven
Workington T.	v.	Huddersfield

Sunday February 25		
Batley	v.	Workington T.
Bramley	v.	Hunslet
Chorley	v.	Ryedale York
Fulham	v.	Doncaster
Halifax	v.	Carlisle
Huddersfield	v.	Dewsbury
Keighley	v.	Oldham
Rochdale H.	v.	Nottingham City
Runcorn H.	v.	Trafford B.
Whitehaven	v.	Hull KR

Sunday March 4		
Carlisle	v.	Dewsbury
Chorley	v.	Halifax
Hull KR.	v.	Keighley
Hunslet	v.	Whitehaven
Oldham	v.	Huddersfield
Runcorn H.	v.	Rochdale H.
Ryedale York	v.	Fulham
Swinton	v.	Batley
Trafford B.	v.	Doncaster
Workington T.	v.	Nottingham City

Sunday March 11		
Batley	v.	Oldham
Bramley	v.	Runcorn H.
Dewsbury	v.	Workington T.
Doncaster	v.	Swinton
Fulham	v.	Huddersfield
Hunslet	v.	Trafford B.
Keighley	v.	Ryedale York
Nottingham City	v.	Carlisle
Rochdale H.	v.	Halifax
Whitehaven	v.	Chorley

Sunday March 18		
Carlisle	v.	Hunslet
Halifax	v.	Batley
Huddersfield	v.	Bramley
Hull KR.	v.	Whitehaven
Nottingham City	v.	Keighley
Oldham	v.	Runcorn H.
Swinton	v.	Dewsbury
Ryedale York	v.	Doncaster
Trafford B.	v.	Fulham
Workington T.	v.	Rochdale H.

Wednesday March 21		
Chorley	v.	Bramley

Sunday March 25		
Batley	v.	Halifax
Bramley	v.	Carlisle
Fulham	v.	Nottingham City
Huddersfield	v.	Oldham
Keighley	v.	Chorley
Rochdale H.	v.	Hunslet
Runcorn H.	v.	Doncaster
Ryedale York	v.	Swinton
Trafford B.	v.	Hull KR.
Workington T.	v.	Dewsbury

Sunday April 1		
Carlisle	v.	Fulham
Chorley	v.	Trafford B.
Dewsbury	v.	Huddersfield
Doncaster	v.	Halifax
Hull KR.	v.	Bramley
Hunslet	v.	Oldham
Nottingham City	v.	Workington T.
Ryedale York	v.	Runcorn H.
Swinton	v.	Rochdale H.
Whitehaven	v.	Batley

Wednesday April 4		
Carlisle	v.	Trafford B.
Hull KR.	v.	Halifax
Swinton	v.	Doncaster

Sunday April 8		
Batley	v.	Hunslet
Fulham	v.	Dewsbury
Halifax	v.	Whitehaven
Huddersfield	v.	Swinton
Nottingham City	v.	Chorley
Oldham	v.	Carlisle
Rochdale H.	v.	Keighley
Runcorn H.	v.	Hull KR.
Workington T.	v.	Doncaster

Wednesday April 11		
Dewsbury	v.	Hull KR.
Halifax	v.	Nottingham City

Good Friday April 13		
Fulham	v.	Chorley
Huddersfield	v.	Halifax
Keighley	v.	Bramley
Rochdale H.	v.	Trafford B.
Ryedale York	v.	Hull KR.
Swinton	v.	Oldham
Whitehaven	v.	Workington T.

Easter Monday April 16		
Bramley	v.	Swinton
Carlisle	v.	Whitehaven
Dewsbury	v.	Fulham
Doncaster	v.	Nottingham City
Halifax	v.	Trafford B.
Hull KR.	v.	Hunslet
Keighley	v.	Huddersfield
Oldham	v.	Rochdale H.
Runcorn H.	v.	Chorley
Ryedale York	v.	Batley